Ancient
Greek Literature

Ancient Greek Literature

K. J. Dover (editor)
E. L. Bowie
Jasper Griffin
M. L. West

Oxford   New York

OXFORD UNIVERSITY PRESS

Oxford University Press, Walton Street, Oxford OX2 6DP

London   New York   Toronto
Delhi   Bombay   Calcutta   Madras   Karachi
Kuala Lumpur   Singapore   Hong Kong   Tokyo
Nairobi   Dar es Salaam   Cape Town
Melbourne   Auckland

and associated companies in
Beirut   Berlin   Ibadan   Mexico City   Nicosia

Oxford is a trade mark of Oxford University Press

First published as an Oxford University Press paperback 1980
and simultaneously in a hardback edition
Reprinted 1985

British Library Cataloguing in Publication Data

Ancient Greek literature. – (Opus).
1. Greek literature – History and criticism
I. Dover, Sir Kenneth James II. Series
880' 9' 001   PA3052   79–41627

ISBN 0–19–219137–3
ISBN 0–19–289124–3 Pbk

Printed in Great Britain by
The Guernsey Press Co Ltd.
Guernsey, Channel Islands

Preface

Since the publication of Sir Maurice Bowra's *Ancient Greek Literature* in 1933, the quantity of Greek literature available to us has been significantly increased by new finds, particularly in respect of lyric poetry and comedy. The activity of scholars in posing new questions and adducing new considerations in order to answer them has brought about some substantial changes in the generally accepted view even of Greek authors who have been studied for a long time. These facts would have justified a revised edition of Bowra's book, but it was decided to replace it by a book of a different kind, in which illustrative quotation from Greek literature would play a much larger part and more account would be taken of the literature of later periods.

Each of us has read and criticized the chapters drafted by the others and has revised his own chapters in the light of criticisms received from them. We do not agree about everything all the time, and none of us should be held responsible for any statement or judgement in a chapter which does not bear his name. Except where otherwise indicated, the writer of each chapter has himself translated the passages which he quotes.

E.L.B.
K.J.D.
J.G.
M.L.W.

Contents

1   Introduction   *K. J. Dover*   1

2   Homeric and Hesiodic poetry   *M. L. West*   10

3   Other early poetry   *M. L. West*   29

4   Tragedy   *K. J. Dover*   50

5   Comedy   *K. J. Dover*   74

6   The classical historians   *K. J. Dover*   88

7   Classical science and philosophy   *K. J. Dover*   105

8   Classical oratory   *K. J. Dover*   122

9   Greek literature 300–50 B.C.   *Jasper Griffin*   134

10   Greek literature after 50 B.C.   *E. L. Bowie*   155

Chronological table   177

Further reading   181

Index   184

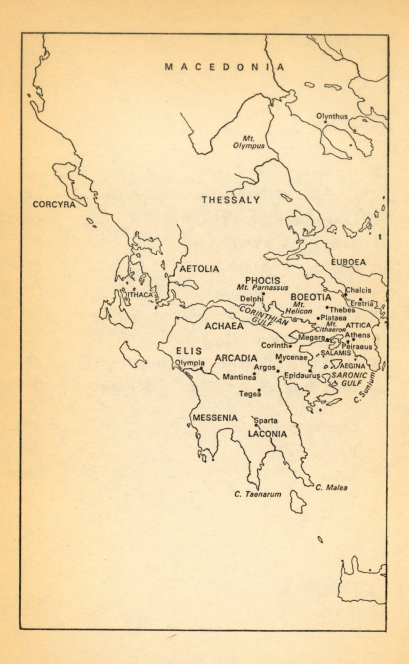

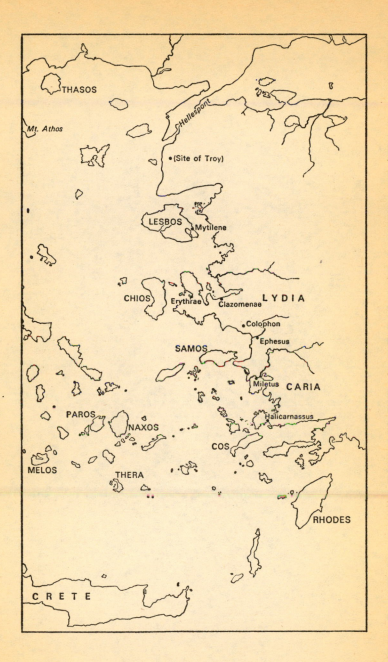

THASOS

Mt. Athos

Hellespont

• (Site of Troy)

LESBOS
Mytilene

CHIOS   Erythrae
Clazomenae   LYDIA

• Colophon
Ephesus

SAMOS

Miletus   CARIA

PAROS
NAXOS   Halicarnassus

MELOS   COS

THERA

RHODES

C R E T E

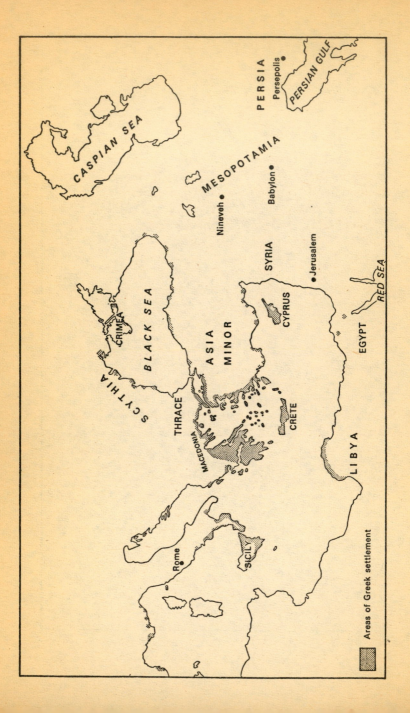

PERSIA

Persepolis

PERSIAN GULF

CASPIAN SEA

MESOPOTAMIA

Babylon

Nineveh

SYRIA

Jerusalem

RED SEA

BLACK SEA

CRIMEA

ASIA MINOR

CYPRUS

SCYTHIA

THRACE

MACEDONIA

CRETE

EGYPT

LIBYA

Rome

SICILY

Areas of Greek settlement

1 Introduction

Greek is not a dead language, as any visitor to Greece (or Melbourne, or Boston) may see and hear for himself. But all languages change all the time, and just as a modern English-speaker cannot read King Alfred's English version of Gregory's *Pastoral Care*, made eleven hundred years ago, unless he has learned 'Old English', so a modern Greek-speaker will not make much headway with Plato's *Phaedo*, written over two thousand three hundred years ago, unless he has learned 'Ancient Greek'. Since languages change steadily, not in sudden leaps, the fixing of boundaries between the 'ancient', 'medieval', and 'modern' stages of a language must be to some extent arbitrary and conventional. In the case of Greek, the advent of Christianity, with the profound cultural changes which this entailed, is a helpful marker, and by common convention (especially in the English-speaking world) 'ancient Greek literature' means the literature which was written in Greek in the pre-Christian centuries, and by non-Christians in the first six centuries of the Christian era. On this criterion the New Testament, although written in Greek in ancient times, is not ancient Greek literature.

Writing was used in Greece and Crete during the Bronze Age, but the written material surviving from that period appears to consist of inventories and other administrative records, not literature. After about 1200 B.C. writing disappeared from the Greek world except, apparently, in Cyprus. Some four hundred years later the Greeks adapted the Phoenician writing-system to create a simple and efficient alphabet, the ultimate ancestor of our own and the Slavonic alphabets. The earliest surviving words in the Greek alphabet are graffiti, often frivolous or indecent, incised on pots or rocks and datable to the neighbourhood of 700 B.C. The Greeks used a variety of writing materials and techniques for different purposes, but literary works were written in ink on papyrus, a fibrous material manufactured in sheets from an Egyptian plant and made up into long rolls by gumming sheets together at the edges.

The earliest Greek literature we have — that is to say, literature composed during the period 700–550 B.C. — is poetry, designed to be sung or recited: narrative about the adventures of ancestral heroes or the achievements and conflicts of gods in an even remoter past; praise and invocation performed by dancing choruses at festivals; moral and practical exhortation; satire, polemic and the expression of personal sentiment in songs suitable for parties or for passing the time.

When we think of Greek literature, it may well be that Greek tragedy is the first thing that comes into our heads. Yet tragedy was a comparatively late arrival on the scene, an invention of the late sixth century B.C.; the earliest tragedy we possess, Aeschylus' *Persians,* was performed in 472. That same period saw the Greeks' tentative exploration of the possibilities of literature in prose, an art-form long familiar to the ancient civilizations of Egypt and the Near East. It was, as it happened, a period of crisis for the Greek world, both internally and externally. Internally, it was marked by the consolidation in certain city-states (notably Athens) of democracy, by which the Greeks meant the taking of political decisions by majority vote in an assembly of all adult male citizens. Externally, it was the period at which the Persian Empire extended its rule to the shores of the Aegean, attempted to subject mainland Greece, and was defeated by Greek courage, skill and good fortune in 480–479 B.C. This crisis marks off the 'archaic' (or 'pre-classical') era of Greek history from the 'classical'. Independently, Greek artists were discovering at this time how to impart grace and fluidity to sculpture in stone. Any causal connection between the defeat of the Persian invasion and contemporaneous developments in politics, art, and literature must, however, be highly speculative, seeing that the crucial steps in those developments had been taken before the Greeks had discovered for sure that they could defend their freedom against Persia.

The Greeks were not a nation governed from a capital city, but a scattering of a thousand city-states on the Greek mainland, the Aegean islands, and parts of the coastline of Turkey, the Black

Sea, Libya, Sicily, and southern Italy. These states were often no bigger in population and territory than a minor English county town, but each asserted its own sovereign status and many were in constant warfare with one another. They were united only by speaking dialects of the same language, by the access to a common literature and culture which that language provided, by participation in shared religious cults and festivals, and by the freedom of movement which their artists and writers enjoyed. In the classical period tragedy was a peculiarly Athenian development, and increasingly admired as the supreme poetic form. This contributed towards turning Athens into the cultural centre of the Greek world, but a more important consideration was the power and wealth which Athens acquired through her role in the defeat of Persia and the imperial control which she exercised over her 'allies' (in effect, subjects) throughout the Aegean. Athens lost this great power when she suffered defeat by Sparta at the end of the fifth century, but no political defeat or humiliation could slow down her increasing domination of culture and literature. It was Athenians who brought prose literature to maturity: Thucydides in history, Plato in philosophy, Demosthenes in oratory. Attic, the dialect of Athens, became the basis of literary and official Greek thereafter and gave rise in its turn to the dialects and stylistic 'registers' of medieval and modern Greek. Nowadays we can often catch ourselves speaking of what 'the Greeks' said or thought, when, if we were more precise, we should realize that we are speaking of the Athenians of the classical period, not of the Greeks as a whole. We need to remind ourselves that in early times Athens was of no special importance in literature (she produced no major poet), and that even in classical times some individuals of great stature in the history of literature — for example, Pindar, Herodotus, and Hippocrates — were not Athenians.

The archaic and classical periods together are the most creative and inventive period of Greek literature; what followed, from about 300 B.C. down to the eclipse of pagan culture by Christianity (300–600 A.D.), was not destitute of invention, but its momentum was reduced and its enterprise circumscribed. The first symptom of decline in poetry was the failure of the fourth century B.C. to take new directions in the composition of tragedy.

At just the time when comedy was alive with experimentation and prose literature was attaining an unsurpassed power and elegance, the Athenians increasingly revived fifth-century trage-dies at their dramatic festivals in preference to the work of new playwrights. Perhaps the loss of their empire engendered in them the feeling that not only the military achievements of the fifth century, but also its characteristic artistic achievements, were beyond emulation; and the City Dionysia, the greatest of the dramatic festivals, was the occasion on which their subject-allies had come annually, and now came no more, to pay their tribute. In the second half of the fourth century not only Athens but the other major cities of Greece and the Aegean suffered an irreversi-ble injury to their confidence when it became clear that the kingdom of Macedonia, under Philip II and his son Alexander the Great, was the arbiter of their fate. Alexander's conquest of the Persian Empire spread the Greek language and culture everywhere in the Near East, but the days of the sovereign city-state were over. In the course of time, all the Greek-speaking areas of the Mediterranean came, step by step, under the rule of Rome. Greek culture of the 'Hellenistic' period — the period, that is to say, after 300 B.C. — could not be wholly immune to nostalgic classicism, and under Roman rule classicism became inordinately strong. To admire great work of the past is one thing, but to deny the possibility of improving on the past is the death of literature. It may be, too, that the artistic ideals of the Greek writer, capable as they were of inspiring swift and dazzling achievement and of discouraging slovenly self-indulgence in experimentation, contained ingredients (for example, preoccupa-tion with human beauty and with traditional stories about deities) which in the end inhibited growth. Whatever the reasons, it is inevitable that a survey of ancient Greek literature which aims at describing and evaluating what was new and fresh and great in it should give more space to the earliest third of its history than to the remaining two-thirds.

Of all that the Greeks wrote, we have no more than a fraction. We know the names of hundreds of Greek historians; we have the work of only three of them from the classical period and a handful from later times. Well over two thousand plays were staged at

Athens between 500 and 200 B.C., but no more than forty-six (two in a badly mutilated condition) are available for us to read or perform. These fearful losses are not attributable to any great natural cataclysm or destructive mania, but principally to a steady decline in interest in pagan literature after the third century A.D. Christianity, naturally enough, diverted intellectual energy from pagan classics into other channels, and set up ideals other than those of literary taste. When a man lost his copy of (say) the poems of Anacreon, he did not trouble to replace it; and that process, multiplied throughout the eastern Mediterranean and prolonged for centuries, was enough to deprive us of almost all ancient Greek literature. That our deprivation is not complete is due above all to the enthusiasm of a few churchmen at Byzantium (Constantinople) in the ninth century A.D., who devoted themselves to rescuing and copying manuscripts of pagan works which still survived here and there from earlier times. From then onwards the study of ancient Greek literature took its place in Byzantine education and culture; western European (particularly Italian) interest in it was awakened in the late Middle Ages and, together with the invention of printing, ensured it a place in our own educational system.

Many surviving works written in Hellenistic times quote, verbatim or in précis, earlier works which are now lost; so it comes about that thanks to anthologies, lexicons, grammatical and metrical treatises, commentaries, and literary or philosophical essays we know something about scores of poems, plays, and books through quotations and excerpts for every one that we can read in its entirety. Indeed, the lost authors about whom we know something far exceed in number those of whom we possess any complete work. Our view of Greek literature is rather like a view of a great mountain range in which a few peaks stand out in perfect clarity against a blue sky while the rest of the range is patchily, tantalizingly hidden by banks and drifts of cloud.

Drifts move; and in modern times excavation of the volcanic deposit which buried Herculaneum and of the dry sand of Egypt has brought to light thousands of fragments of copies of texts actually produced in Hellenistic times. They range from the meagre (a few unintelligible syllables) to the magnificent (a whole play), and they have given us not only works otherwise lost (notably comedies of Menander, lyric poems of Bacchylides, and Aristotle's *Constitution of Athens*) but also portions of already known texts very much older than the earliest complete copies of those texts. For example, the oldest complete text of Plato's *Phaedo* is contained in a Byzantine manuscript written in 895 A.D., nearly thirteen hundred years after the work was composed, but some substantial fragments of a papyrus copy from Egypt take us back to within a century of Plato's own lifetime. There is no reason why the discovery of papyri should not continue indefinitely; ancient Greek literature is not a body of material fixed for all time by what survived from the ancient to the medieval world, but increases every year, and naturally our knowledge of the Greek language and other aspects of Greek civilization increases with it. Moreover, practically all the literature which was rescued from oblivion in the early Middle Ages owed its survival to a process of selection — it represents what was most admired and most often read and studied in the last centuries of the Roman Empire. But papyri reflect the taste of earlier centuries, at any rate in one area of the Mediterranean, and are essentially (what is always valuable to a student of any literature) samples preserved by chance. The taste of the late Roman Empire was not, of course, wholly alien from ours or from that of the classical era itself, and no one will carp at its preference for Sophocles over Morsimus or for Plato over Aeschines of Sphettus, but it is legitimate to wonder whether we, whittling down the seventy tragedies of Aeschylus to seven, would have chosen precisely those seven which have in fact survived.

In ancient and medieval times every copy of a text had to be made, by a hand wielding a pen, from another; and since it is very hard to copy a complete text without making a single slip, and very easy to insert in an individual copy words which were no part of the author's intention, it is not surprising that we never find two manuscript copies of the same Greek text which are in total agreement throughout. Ancient systems of correcting errors, rectifying omissions, and adding explanatory notes were, moreover, deficient in clarity and precision. All these hazards beset a work from the very moment when it left its author's hands, as the ancients themselves recognized. Choosing between alternatives, deciding when words have been omitted or added, and forming defensible opinions on what the author probably wrote in cases where the only available manuscripts present us with something dubious or nonsensical, are the business of textual criticism. Textual problems are always literary and linguistic problems as well, and sometimes also historical problems; the study of ancient literature is not easily divisible into separate compartments. The modern scholar-critic-editor has to do the same kind of job as the ancient Greek scholars who edited Homer or Pindar in the third and second centuries B.C., but he can often do the job better, for although he knows much less about some things, he knows more about others. It could be said, paradoxically, that he has the benefit of two thousand years more experience. Textual problems seldom matter to those who enjoy Greek literature only in translation, but now and again an issue of content is at stake; it makes a difference, for example, whether Demosthenes (xxiii 205) said that Kimon subverted 'our inherited constitution' (*tēn patrion polīteiān*) or that he subverted 'the constitution of Paros' (*tēn Pariōn polīteiān*), because the passage exemplifies the beliefs of fourth-century Athenians about the earlier history of their own democracy, and one wants to know what belief is exemplified here.

The question 'But how do we know what any of it *means*?' is one of those naïve-sounding but fundamental questions which no one should be ashamed to ask; after all, we would ask it unhesitatingly about (say) Elamite. There are, of course, some constants in Greek; *tí* meant 'what?' to Homer and it still means 'what?' But fortunately we do not have to decipher ancient texts solely on the basis of the modern spoken language, for Greek has continuously been both a medium of literature and an object of study. From early Hellenistic times onwards Greeks wrote commentaries on the literature which they had inherited; they compiled glossaries and discussed grammar; and the tradition of systematic study and interpretation was continued at Byzantium. Hence, although we may all have to admit defeat when confronted by a temple inventory on an archaic inscription in a little-known dialect, the reader of Greek literature in translation need not fear that different translators, however they differ in style and in their conception of a translator's job, are constantly guessing and disagreeing about what the author meant to say.

The reader himself will find some kinds of Greek literature harder than others. The comedies of Aristophanes and many speeches of the orators are full of topicalities and technicalities familiar enough to the audiences for whom they were composed but needing nowadays explanatory comment which tends to bleed a joke of its humour and a sarcastic argument of its force. What, one might ask, would Aristophanes make of a modern joke which turned on the phrase 'Government Warning' and the importance of tobacco to the Budget? On the other hand, epic, tragedy, historical narrative, and philosophical dialogue speak directly to our imagination and experience, once we have learned (the task of a day, perhaps) to change gear smoothly from monotheism or scepticism into polytheism and back again.

We find in ancient Greek literature the expression of some moral, social, and religious values which are distinctively and characteristically Greek, and we observe an indifference to some modern preoccupations, such as 'human rights' and 'diminished responsibility'. This is not at all the same as saying that they were indifferent to cruelty, did not value freedom, or were not interested in the determinants of behaviour. We must, however, be cautious in generalizing about '*the* Greek view' of any specific issue, for the Greeks were just as much individual human beings as we are; at the height of the classical period primitive superstition coexisted with radical scepticism and rigid convention with adventurous speculation, for in general the Greeks were accustomed to speak their minds and did not readily defer to temporal or spiritual authority. In science and technology they were nearer to the Stone Age than they are to us, but in perception and understanding of humanity they were our equals, and, to judge from the poetry and oratory addressed to mass audiences, the average Greek compares very favourably in taste and sensitivity with his counterpart in any other known civilization.

Greek literature was created by a succession of brilliant innovations, but every innovation was a graft on to a firmly rooted stock, and the pace of change, although fast by the standards of Ancient Egypt and Babylonia, was slow in comparison with what we have experienced in our own century. Since the Greeks wrote very little about art or literature (except oratory) our understanding of their attitude to the arts must depend on inference seasoned with intuition, but it is clear that they did not value experimentation as such; they waited to see what the experiment amounted to. Nor did they value self-expression for its own sake, but considered the quality of the self which was being expressed, and despised expression which was deficient in artistic discipline and skill. Nor, again, did they attempt to assess a writer's 'sincerity'; literature, like shoemaking or bonesetting, was classified as a *tekhnē,* in which structured procedures had to be learned, and any exercise of a *tekhnē* is judged by how it works. Modern literary criticism of any work of Greek literature may go badly astray if it does not begin by considering the place of that work in the history of the genre to which it belongs and the extent to which it retains or modifies the formal structure characteristic of that genre.

There is no sign that the Greeks thought that any art had an obligation to be charged with despair or to depict squalor because the society for which it was created was afflicted by despair or beset by squalor. They are more likely to have concurred with the view that it is the business of the arts to compensate for life by creating what life generally fails to create: people of extraordinary beauty and courage, moments divested of all triviality. A modern painter said: 'I paint like a barbarian, in a barbarous age.' A Greek might have retorted: 'If your age is barbarous, that is the strongest possible reason for not painting like a barbarian.'

2 Homeric and Hesiodic poetry

If Greek literature first appears in the eighth century B.C., the reason is simply that that was when the Greeks learned alphabetic writing from the Phoenicians. They had not by any means been without literature during the preceding centuries of illiteracy. All peoples at all times have poetry, song, and storytelling, whether or not they have writing, and it may safely be asserted, on more than one ground, that the earliest Greek poetry we have is the matured product of many hundreds of years of evolution. We must not think of Greek literature as *beginning* in the eighth century but as *coming into view*.

The Greeks did not immediately start writing down everything they composed in prose and verse. They did not, to begin with, think in terms of addressing posterity: one sang or recited for the occasion, to entertain an audience or to please the gods. With some kinds of composition — drama and oratory are obvious examples — the oral performance was always primary, and written circulation secondary. The same is true of all lyric poetry down to the fourth century B.C., and of most other poetry down to the early fifth century. There must have been much that was never written down, and what was written still became known more from being heard than from being read. We cannot reckon with the existence of a sizeable reading public until the latter part of the fifth century at Athens, and probably later in many parts of Greece.

The dates at which different types of literature began to be written down are well spread out. What seemed of permanent or universal value was recorded earlier than what was local and ephemeral. Poetry preceded prose by nearly two centuries, because in the early period whatever was intended to endure was put in poetic form; and poetry of substantial content, epic and wisdom poetry, appeared earlier than poetry of other kinds.

When prose compositions began to appear, from about 550, they were at first limited to disquisitions on serious subjects like cosmology, history, geography, and architectural technique. At Athens texts of tragedies began to circulate about 500, whereas comedy, which had origins no less ancient, did not achieve literary status for another half century. Oratory surfaced even later, though men had always harangued assemblies and pleaded cases at law. Of course not all branches of literature are of equal antiquity; but we must not judge their age simply by when they first appeared in written form.

Epic poetry certainly goes back much earlier than the *Iliad* and *Odyssey* and the other written epics that gained currency in the archaic period. All these poems look back to events supposed to have happened a dozen or more generations previously, when Mycenae, Tiryns, Pylos, Iolkos were important towns, and Thebes and Troy were sacked. This heroic age of epic tradition contains a hard core of historical reality. Archaeology confirms that the towns remembered in epic (and in Greek mythology generally) as being rich and powerful actually were so in the Mycenaean age, down to the thirteenth or twelfth century B.C., and in most cases never achieved such status again. Troy really was destroyed by human violence in the thirteenth century, and Thebes a little earlier. It is true that archaeology cannot tell us whether the personalities and events described in the epic tradition are historical, and while some of them may be, the analogy of those medieval and modern European epic traditions which can be controlled from historical records teaches us plainly that we must reckon with all kinds of distortion, exaggeration, contamination of unconnected stories, transfer of motifs, and fictional embellishment. Men who lived in different centuries may be represented as contemporaries, traitors turned into heroes, defeats into victories. Troy may have been sacked by Greeks, but it is very unlikely to have been by a vast confederacy from all parts of Greece and the islands, filling over a thousand ships. Nor was it sacked on account of Helen, who appears to have been in origin a goddess and not a real person at all. Most of the heroes named in the epics about the war were probably historical personages, but if so they may have lived at various different times and been originally remembered for things that had nothing to do with the Trojan saga. But granting all this, it is clear that the epic tradition does enshrine some genuine memories from the second millennium. Besides the major facts of political geography, it preserves descriptions of arms and armour of types assignable to that time — some of it, indeed, already out of fashion by the time Troy fell — and it generally represents the heroes as using swords and spearheads of bronze, although after the coming of iron-working to Greece in the eleventh century they were commonly made of iron. The Homeric language itself preserves many very ancient words and grammatical forms which were obsolete in historical times. We have evidently to assume not just 'folk memories' from the late Mycenaean age, but a continuous *poetic* tradition reaching back to that time, or at any rate to a time not very much more recent, a tradition of which Homer is a comparatively late representative.

This tradition must have been exclusively oral in its earlier phases, as Greece was illiterate until the eighth century. The *Iliad* and *Odyssey*, written poems though they are, show many signs of an oral ancestry. The poet summons the Muse at the beginning to 'tell' or 'sing' him the story. The Muses know everything that happened, but we mortals only 'hear the report' of it. The heroes are entertained by bards who 'sing' of famous deeds on request and without special preparation, accompanying themselves on the lyre. The epic language and style were clearly formed under conditions like those in which popular heroic poetry has been composed and orally maintained in more recent times in Yugoslavia, Russia, and elsewhere. Each performer learns the traditional stories by listening to other performers (sometimes also from written collections, where literacy exists), and he learns a traditional style in which to tell them. He does not necessarily try to add anything new when he himself performs, but it is easier for him to re-tell the tale in verses of his own, each time he tells it, than to reproduce what he has heard word for word. He makes much use of formulaic phrases handed down from one poet to another and repeated as often as convenient, and he shows little desire for originality of expression. Nor does he cultivate metrical variety: he uses a single stereotyped verse which is repeated over and over again till the story is finished. Repeated scenes and motifs are a conspicuous feature of the narrative. Homeric epic bears the marks of this kind of oral tradition. Every reader notices the constantly reiterated formulae (at least in the Greek; translations often play them down): 'fleet-footed Achilles', 'Zeus the cloud-gatherer', 'black ships', 'windy Troy', the epithets often irrelevant to the context and occasionally inappropriate to it; 'answered and addressed him'; 'while he pondered this in his heart and mind'. He notices too how the narrative is punctuated, steadied, by routine occurrences of no dramatic significance in themselves: dawn, people rising and dressing, baths, meals, sacrifices, sunset, going to bed, each related in typical verses which might be used in any epic. Recurrent themes such as the arming of a warrior, a chariot journey, a sea voyage, are dealt with methodically according to a standard programme. That is to say, for each such scene there is a basic sequence of details that the poet takes in order, however much he may enlarge on them or vary his expression at the verbal level. These are different aspects of a technique which enabled the practised oral poet to tell any story in a reasonably fluent and orderly fashion.

The Homeric epics, then, are very much in the style of the oral tradition which lay behind them. Their authors were almost certainly men skilled as oral performers, men for whom recitation was the norm and the production of a written version an exceptional undertaking. What they wrote was based on what they recited. However, we cannot regard the written texts simply as transcripts of oral performances. Each recitation was a kind of re-creation; the writing-down must have been, too — a more radical re-creation, because it was done at leisure over a long period, with no limit of length set by the patience of an audience, and nothing to prevent going back and changing a passage already composed. Such changes do occasionally appear to have been made. The *Iliad* came out at some fifteen thousand lines, the *Odyssey* at some twelve thousand. That their authors had been accustomed to recite poems of this length, as serials over a period of days, is theoretically possible, but there is no reason at all to assume it. Both stories could have been told effectively in much shorter compass. The *Iliad* poet seems in fact to be incorporating several different items from his repertoire in his great book, while the *Odyssey* poet sometimes seems to be seeking length for its own sake. Other early epics of which we have knowledge (none of them now surviving) were much shorter.

To speak of 'the *Iliad* poet' and 'the *Odyssey* poet' is, of course, to take up a position on the Homeric Question — the question whether both poems had the same author, and whether either of them had a single author. The majority of Homeric scholars now accept that each poem is substantially the creation of one poet, but regard the differences of style and compositional technique as too great to allow the attribution of both to the same author. Everyone in antiquity (except for one or two heretics whose arguments, so far as we know them, were trivial) ascribed them both to Homer. No alternative candidate is heard of, unless we count a tale that Homer collected the material for the *Odyssey* at a time of his life when his name was Melesigenes, before he came to be called Homer. But the consensus of antiquity is not strong evidence. The ancients abhorred anonymity as nature abhors a vacuum, and a composition whose author was unknown — as was the case with a number of early epics — would readily be ascribed to the most celebrated author of the appropriate type. Homer was actually credited with many more poems than the *Iliad* and *Odyssey*. The arguments from style and technique carry greater weight. Some of the differences will be mentioned in what follows.

One point on which we must accept the verdict of antiquity is the superiority of the *Iliad* and *Odyssey* to the other, shorter epics. The very few fragments that we possess of those poems suggest that the ancients were right. We also have plot summaries for six epics concerned with the Trojan War and associated events, part of the so-called Epic Cycle. It appears that some of them quite lacked unity and merely related a succession of events in an episodic manner. The most interesting was perhaps the *Aethiopis*, the epic that culminated in the death of Achilles. It seems to have been better constructed than most, and the poet of the *Iliad* clearly knew, if not the *Aethiopis* itself, something that had much in common with it; the comparison would have been highly instructive.

II

The *Iliad* is the supreme monument of ancient epic poetry. If Homer was the best poet, we must ascribe it to him. Set against a background of war, the traditional theatre of heroic achievement, and full of battle scenes as it is, it transcends martial epic by its sense of the pity of war. Homer is not simply celebrating the triumph of Greeks over Trojans, pandering to national pride. His sympathy is with the doomed and dying of both sides. It is a drama of human passions that forms the main plot. The climax is the death of Hector, Troy's great champion, at the hands of Achilles: a heroic accomplishment in itself, but given immensely greater human significance by being made an act of personal vengeance for the killing of Achilles' dearest friend, Patroclus, and by the dramatic portrayal of Hector's alternating courage and fear, the agony of his parents who watch helplessly from the city wall, and the grief of family and people as they prepare to bury their hope. The death of Patroclus is itself the consequence of a chain of personal acts prompted by clear-cut, universal emotions. Forced by the anger of Apollo to release a girl captive from among his personal trophies, Agamemnon demands a replacement, for if he loses a trophy, he loses prestige, and prestige above all is what a Homeric hero lives for. This leads to a quarrel with Achilles and the decision to take a girl from him. Both girls, incidentally, are loved by their masters: inanimate trophies would have served the poet's purpose, but he prefers the additional personal factor. Achilles henceforth stays out of battle so that the Trojans may gain the upper hand and the Greeks be forced to restore him to honour. Eventually the situation becomes so critical that he allows Patroclus to go out to fight in his, Achilles', armour, so that the Trojans think it is he. But Patroclus trusts his luck too far and falls to Hector.

We cannot tell how far Homer has developed these personal and emotional aspects of his narrative beyond what he inherited from his predecessors. But he must in any event be judged an artist with rare depths of humanity. Typical of him is the scene where Hector visits his wife and infant son in the city — the child whose only destiny was to be thrown to his death from the walls by the victors. Andromache, afraid that she will soon be a widow,

as indeed she will be, pleads tearfully with Hector not to go back
to the field. But he dare not be thought a coward, and in any case
it is his nature to seek glory in the front line.

'Well I know in heart and spirit:
there shall come a day when holy
Ilios at last shall perish,
Priam too and Priam's people;
yet I grieve less for the Trojans,
even Hecuba and Priam
and my many noble brothers
falling in the dust to foemen,
than for you, when some Achaean
warrior takes you off in tears,
robs you of your days of freedom:
at some Argive lady's loom then
will you weave, or carry water
from Messeïs or Hyperia,
not from choice but harsh compulsion.
They will say who see your tears,
'That one was the wife of Hector,
who was bravest of the Trojans
when they fought for holy Ilios'.
So they'll say, and your pain sharpen
that I am not there to save you.
But I pray to die, lie buried
under earth, before I hear you
being carried off and crying.'
(*Iliad* vi 447–65)

This passage comes a quarter of the way through the poem; but
Homer probably did not know, when he composed it, how much
longer his poem would become. The course of the narrative up to
this point suggests that the Greek crisis and Hector's death will
come much sooner than they actually do. The scene between
Hector and Andromache may have been conceived as a prelude
to his death. It is a feature of epic composition that the poet
prepares for every important turn of events in advance by means
of prophecies, portents, debates, proposals, decisions of the gods.
We know by the end of the first book that the Trojans are to gain
the upper hand and Achilles be restored to full honour, because
Zeus has promised Thetis, Achilles' divine mother, that it will be

so. He promises it because she asks him to, and that is the consequence of a conversation between her and Achilles. It is on her advice that Achilles withdraws from the fighting. In the next book hundreds of lines are devoted to bringing the Greeks to the point of going into battle, which one might expect them to do as a matter of routine. Zeus has to send Agamemnon a special dream to encourage him. Agamemnon has to confer with his counsellors and then with the army; there have to be sacrifices and prayers; even then Nestor has to *propose* to Agamemnon that he *tell* the heralds to *order* the army to form up, and all these steps are gone through. The gathering of the army is embellished with a series of detailed similes and then with a lengthy catalogue of contingents. The vast length of the epics is due in no small part to this kind of preparatory elaboration. It means that we can see quite well what the poet has in mind for later, where he has changed his plan, and where he has enlarged it, postponing some well-prepared event in order to insert a new episode. The structure and proportions of the *Iliad* do suffer somewhat from these insertions, especially from extra battle episodes in which Homer seems temporarily to forget his goal. But he always comes back in the end to the plan which he has laid out for himself and crystallized as Zeus' plan. We notice a shift of perspective as the poem develops. It begins as the story of 'the wrath of Achilles', which caused the Greeks such great losses. The wrath ends in reconciliation, but by that time we have the death of Hector in view. Towards the end there are increasingly frequent and clear references to Achilles' own coming death, as if Homer envisaged going further and crowning his gigantic work with an even greater climax.

The gods are in general not an expression of the poet's religious beliefs but part of his mechanism for preparing future events. Much of what happens can be traced back to their initiative. Yet it is really governed not by them but by unalterable tradition or the poet's designs: the gods are his puppets, and must do whatever the story demands. If Athena lends her strength to a spear-throw, it hits its mark; if she deflects the spear in its flight, it misses; but which she does is determined by whether the story requires the man aimed at to survive. The ebb and flow of battle, the alternate dominance of opposed forces, presupposes opposition between gods. Over and above the ebb and flow looms the final outcome; and this has its theological counterpart in the will of Zeus, which the lesser gods may misconstrue or oppose but cannot in the end thwart, because it is identical with the poet's will. To heighten the pathos when Sarpedon and again when Hector dies, Homer can represent even Zeus as wavering, tempted to spare the doomed man: the poet's will then assumes the guise of Fate, against which even Zeus cannot struggle. He can also use the gods simply to raise the action to a higher plane. Diomedes' extraordinary supremacy in books v–vi is underlined by allowing gods to face him in battle and retire discomfited, and the last great battle before Hector is killed is made more sensational by the participation of eleven divinities who actually fight one another.

Although his narrative outgrows itself at times, in general Homer keeps it remarkably well under control. He may forget after a long interval that a minor character has been killed, but he is skilful at interlacing separate strands of action and remembering where everyone is and what they were about when last mentioned. He is conscious of the need to introduce his cast to us. The catalogue of contingents in book ii, the scene where Helen points out the Greek heroes to Priam in book iii, and Agamemnon's review of his commanders in book iv, all tend to serve this purpose, and other characters such as Calchas, Nestor, Thersites, are introduced in their place. Homer has a clear and consistent concept of the individual personalities of his principal heroes: the young Achilles has the keenest emotional reactions, Odysseus is canny and persuasive, Diomedes brave and cheerful, and so on. It is through their speeches above all that their characters appear. Homer has the gift of throwing himself into each part, feeling their feelings and speaking with their voices. The masterly account of the quarrel between Achilles and Agamemnon, with the two proud men provoking each other further with each reply, may serve as an example of his dramatic art.

It has been mentioned that the Homeric language is rich in archaisms of grammar and vocabulary. This does not mean that it would have been found hard to understand. Epic recitation was among the most popular forms of entertainment at public and private gatherings, and the audiences were familiar enough with the language to understand it as well as the bards did themselves. Syntax and word order were straightforward, metaphors few and conventional, new coinages transparent. The ornament of style in which the poets gave most play to their originality was the extended simile. The *Iliad* is especially notable for the number and brilliance of its similes. Many examples clamour for quotation; but let the following portrayal of the tense quietness of night before renewed battle, with the Trojans now daring to camp outside their wall, serve to exemplify at once Homer's talent for simile and his powers of description.

> They in pride on battle's bridges
> sat all through the night, and many
> were the fires they had burning.
> As the stars shine round the bright moon
> brilliant, when the air is windless:
> all the peaks and glens and ridges
> stand out clear, and under heaven
> shear off sharp the endless ether;
> all the stars are there for seeing,
> and the shepherd's heart rejoices:-
> e'en so many shone the fires
> that the Trojans there had burning,
> from the ships to Xanthos' waters,
> on the plain before the city.
> There a thousand fires were burning,
> and by each sat fifty warriors
> in the gleaming of the firelight;
> and their horses champing barley,
> champing groats beside their chariots,
> stood and waited for the morning.
>
> (*Iliad* viii 553–65)

III

The *Odyssey*'s virtues are different. Instead of a tragedy of heroic passions set against a background of semi-historical saga, it is a story of one man's triumph over adversity in a world of folk-tale — folk-tale that has been tacked on to the traditions about the Trojan War to justify its inclusion in the province of epic poetry.

Odysseus of Ithaca is presumably a historical figure in origin, but nothing that happens to him in the *Odyssey* can be assumed to have a historical basis. The episodes in which he is involved would be equally exciting and interesting whoever they happened to, prince or peasant; and that is the essence of a folk-tale, that it circulates because it is a good story, whoever it happened to, and attaches itself to different characters at different times. One of the most certain results of Homeric scholarship is that a whole series of Odysseus' adventures at sea have been transferred to him from the legend of the Argonauts. The poet himself indicates in one case that he knows the story in connection with them. We can hardly avoid the conclusion that he or one of his immediate predecessors made this wholesale transfer quite consciously, as a deliberate device to add to the number of Odysseus' exploits. Others of them are well attested in European and Asiatic folklore, or contain motifs that are. Several have no particular connection with the sea. Some call for a party of men, others for a man by himself, and the narrative has to be adjusted accordingly. Even the story of Penelope's suitors, which seems firmly set in the real world, must on sober consideration be judged fabulous. Here again there are widespread parallels in folklore, the most detailed being from the Turkic peoples of the Altai region, who are unlikely to have been influenced by the *Odyssey*. The story requires Odysseus, who is not among those who use the bow in the *Iliad,* to be a mighty archer — an archer who leaves his bow at home when he goes to war. And although more than half the *Odyssey* is concerned with the suitors, there are one or two passages suggesting that once Odysseus surmounts the difficulties of the voyage to Ithaca, he will find everything peaceful at home and his adventures will be over.

Inconsistencies are characteristic of the poem, only they tend to be consistent with each other in a way that suggests submerged earlier versions. It looks as if the poet was an inventive man who was capable of altering his narrative quite radically between one recitation and another, and in the course of producing his written poem, without always covering his traces. But it also seems that the poem has suffered more than the *Iliad* from later revision of the written text, affecting particularly the ending and also some other passages. It is unlikely that scholars will ever agree on the details, but many have come to similar conclusions.

The story has a much greater span in space and time than that of the *Iliad,* but the poet gives it a tight structure by putting the ten years of wanderings in the form of a first-person account in Odysseus' mouth, thus concentrating his own narrative within a few weeks, and by ambitious use of the interlacing technique, so that we get a clear picture of action going forward simultaneously in different regions of the world. There are three great strands, eventually woven together: Odysseus at sea; the suitors at Ithaca; and Telemachus journeying in search of news of his father. Telemachus' visits at Pylos and Sparta enable us to hear about the returns of other heroes from Troy and thus to see Odysseus' return in a fuller context at the outset of the poem. There is repeated reference to the heroic deed of Orestes, who avenged his father Agamemnon by killing his mother's lover: he is held up as a model for Telemachus to follow, and various passages might suggest that the poet at one time thought of having Telemachus kill the suitors just before his father's return. If so, we see again how ready he is to borrow themes from other stories — and to change his mind.

His interest in people is different from that of the poet of the *Iliad.* He is less concerned with the variety and intensity of their feelings than with how sensible and good or foolish and bad they are. The whole poem is to do with the victory of good and the punishment of wickedness; the poet is interested in morality, and so are his gods. He does not limit his gaze to the hero class: important parts are played by menials, and there is little trace of the aristocratic confusion of social standing with absolute quality which we find in some other early Greek poetry (though it is true that the loyal nurse and swineherd are both of good birth). We spend some time, indeed, in the lowly surroundings of the swineherd's hut. The poet's imagination seems to be as much at home there, or in Laertes' vineyard, as in the palace.

He has a lively sense of topography and an accompanying talent for description both of human constructions, such as Alcinous' mansion and town, and of natural scenery. The Greeks' appreciation of nature in the archaic and classical periods is sometimes underrated, perhaps because they have left no poems or essays devoted to it. Greek literature is predominantly anthropocentric. Nevertheless there are many passages which testify to their awareness of natural beauty, and nowhere more than in the *Odyssey*. For instance, when Hermes is sent to Calypso's island to tell her to send Odysseus on his way, the conventional programme for messengers' journeys requires the poet to say that the god arrived at her cave and found her, and what he found her doing. But our poet then inserts ten lines (v. 63–72) describing the surrounding scenery, and ties it in to his narrative by making Hermes pause and admire it before delivering his message.

Elegant modification of standard procedures is one of the poet's characteristics. One further example must suffice. Instead of Menelaus or Helen asking Telemachus who he is, as is customary with visitors, Helen voices to her husband her conjecture that it is the son of Odysseus (so great is the likeness), and Menelaus agrees that there is reason to think so; Telemachus' travelling companion confirms it (iv. 137 ff.). Not exactly like real life, yet the participants in this free-moving dialogue seem extraordinarily lifelike figures who have adapted the epic language to their own colloquial purposes.

Unfortunately the *Odyssey* poet's fluency is not always so effective. After the action-filled first half of the poem, the second half seems disproportionately long for the amount of event in it, particularly books xiv–xx. It is the epic manner that action should be hedged about with dialogue, but here there is too much dialogue that is not organically related to the action. Perhaps, as has been suggested, the poet is striving after amplitude for its own sake. It is very probable that he knew the *Iliad,* and he may have wanted to emulate its enormous bulk. But his method of creating bulk is quite different. He is content to dwell on static situations of all kinds, and especially men at ease telling each other stories — the setting in which he himself was most at home. The successful, honoured bards portrayed in the *Odyssey,* Phemius and Demodocus, reflect his own ideal.

IV

One of Demodocus' lays is a tale not about heroes but about gods: the merry tale of the adultery of Ares and Aphrodite, and

how her husband Hephaestus caught them in a specially manufactured trap. Stories of this sort, and more solemn myths about
the gods, were related in the epic style in poems of up to a few
hundred lines in length, often by way of a preface to a heroic
poem. It was the custom of the rhapsode to begin his performance
with an address to a god; it might be a brief invocation of only a
few lines, or it might be much longer, with a narrative core. The
so-called Homeric Hymns are a collection of about thirty such
preludes, collectively ascribed to Homer but in fact composed in
different parts of Greece at different dates, probably ranging from
the second half of the seventh century to the first half of the fifth.
They are hymns in that they celebrate gods, often include
description of their characteristic activities and powers, and
generally end with a direct salutation. Their earliest attested
name, however, is *prooimion,* meaning 'what precedes the *hoimē,*
the main theme', referring to their prefatory function. They
mostly end with a formula of transition such as

> Farewell, goddess, queen of Cyprus:
> having made thee my beginning,
> I'll pass on to other singing.
> (*Hymn* v 292–3)

Some of the poets pray for success and prosperity, or that they
will give a good performance; one asks for 'victory in this
competition' (vi. 19).

The finest of the longer hymns, the closest to Homer in style,
and probably the oldest, is the *Hymn to Aphrodite.* It tells the story
of the goddess's seduction of the Trojan Anchises. The child she
will bear, Aeneas, is represented (as also in the *Iliad*) as the
ancestor of a dynasty that will rule in Troy in later generations,
after its sack by the Greeks, and continue indefinitely. This
presumably refers to the Aeolian settlement at Troy, Ilios,
established a little before 700 B.C.; its ruling house evidently
claimed descent from Aeneas, and the myth of Aphrodite and
Anchises must therefore have had special importance for them.
The hymn may well have been composed for their ears. The
Hymns to Demeter and Apollo, too, are connected with particular local interests. The Demeter hymn gives the foundation myth
of the Eleusinian Mysteries, those increasingly popular religious

ceremonies, celebrated annually at Eleusis in Attica, which promised the initiate a happy fate after death. The Hymn to Apollo is a fusion of two separate hymns, both attributable to the sixth century. One is about Apollo's birth on the island of Delos, and was composed for a festival on Delos. (The poet reveals that he comes from Chios, and is blind, which no doubt underlies the later belief that Homer was blind.) The other is centred on Delphi, and tells how Apollo first came there and established his temple and priesthood. We can safely assume that it was composed at Delphi or at least intended for performance there. The *Hymn to Hermes* has no such obvious local connection. It is almost certainly the latest at least of the long hymns, but its theme, the amusing pranks of the baby Hermes, strikes a similar note to Demodocus' lay of Ares and Aphrodite. Among the shorter hymns, those to Dionysus (vii) and Pan (xix) are of particular interest.

V

The 'Homeric' poetry we have been considering up to now comprises heroic narrative poems and the pieces that served to preface them. Beside it there existed poetry in the same language and hexameter metre which does not fit into that category and which is particularly associated with the name of Hesiod. Some of it was narrative, but differed from Homeric epic in that its aim was not the exciting or entertaining relation of a particular story, but the systematic coverage, the codification, of a whole area of tradition, such as the genealogies of the heroes and heroines of various parts of Greece, all linked in common descent from Hellēn, the mythical eponym of the Hellenic nation. Other 'Hesiodic' poems were didactic, embodying moral and practical instruction of various kinds.

We possess two genuine works by Hesiod, one from each of the categories mentioned; whether any of the other poems attributed to him in antiquity was authentic is uncertain. In both he tells us something about himself, and consequently he is much more real a figure for us than is Homer, whose most basic personal particulars were a matter of dispute from quite early times.

Hesiod lived at Ascra, an upland village in Boeotia, his father having migrated there from Aeolian Cyme on the other side of the Aegean, where he had pursued an unprofitable career as a sea trader. In the earlier of the two poems, the *Theogony*, Hesiod claims that as he was tending sheep below Mount Helicon he heard the Muses speaking to him, and they gave him a staff of bay, endowed him with skill at poetry, and told him to sing of the family of gods. The *Theogony* is the fulfilment of their command. Its subject is the gods' origin and genealogies, and the events that led to the establishment of the present world order. The gods include not only the conventional figures of cult but the divine world-masses Sea, Sky, Mountains, etc., and abstract entities of permanent significance in human life, whose connections the genealogical form expresses neatly:

> Strife gave birth to grievous Toil,
> Neglect, Starvation, woeful Pain,
> Wars and Battles, Bloodshed, Slaughter,
> Quarrels, Lies, Pretences and Arguments,
> Crime and Derangement, neighbours twain,
> and Oath, who punishes men most,
> when one is knowingly forsworn.
> (Hesiod, *Theogony* 226–32)

The genealogies, which embrace some three hundred names, are interlaced with passages of somewhat less fluent narrative, mainly to do with the succession of rulers in heaven: the castration of Uranos by Kronos, and the overthrow of Kronos and the Titans by Zeus and the Olympian gods. The passage where Hesiod speaks of his poetic initiation comes in a prefatory hymn to the Muses, analogous to a Homeric Hymn.

The *Works and Days* might be better entitled 'the Wisdom of Hesiod'. It is a moral-didactic poem of mixed content, formally addressed to the poet's erring brother Perses and to the local rulers who have shown Perses undue favour, but intended for the edification of the general public. In the first part the addressees are exhorted to deal righteously, and Perses also to work for his bread. In the second part the rulers disappear; as for Perses, it is assumed that he accepts the advice of the first part, and he is given instruction on how to farm and also on seafaring, in case he wants to sell his surplus produce elsewhere. There is other

material that does not fit into this general plan: rules for conduct
in various social contexts, interesting religious taboos, days of the
month that are favourable or unfavourable for different purposes.
As he added to his poem, Hesiod seems to have come to conceive
it as a general compendium of useful advice. Even Perses fades
out well before the end.

Many of Hesiod's precepts must be traditional. In places they
come thick and fast, one following another into his mind:

> Avoid base gains: base gains amount to losses.
> Be friend to friend, companion to companion.
> Give him, who gives, and give him not, who gives not:
> one gives to giver, gives not to non-giver.
> Give is good, but Snatch is bad, death-giving.
> For if a man gives willing, even much,
> he is glad at the gift, his heart rejoices,
> but if the other takes it for himself,
> even a mite, that turns his mood to frost.
> For if you stack but a mite upon a mite,
> and do it oft, e'en that may well grow great.
>
> (Hesiod, *Works and Days* 352–62)

But he has a variety of other means of expression: remonstrance,
warnings of divine anger, animal fable, myths explaining why the
world is as it is. There is a fine, though quaint, descriptive
passage about the effects of winter on the earth and its creatures.
Hesiod's poetry is often memorable, even if more for particular
visual images and for pungent formulations which may not be
original to him than for sustained power or beauty. Yet the *Works
and Days* in particular is a fascinating document of one stratum of
archaic life and thought.

As our knowledge of the literatures of the Near East (particularly Sumerian-Akkadian and Hittite) has grown in the present
century, it has been increasingly realized that Hesiod, more than
any other early Greek poet, derives much — no doubt indirectly
— from oriental sources. The Succession Myth in the *Theogony*
shows detailed similarities to older Babylonian and Hurrian
myths and is unquestionably related to them somehow. There is
reason to think that the myth of the five races of men in the *Works
and Days* — the golden race, the silver, and the rest — and the
doctrine of propitious and unpropitious days of the month are

also of Eastern, perhaps Mesopotamian provenance. And the poem as a whole has its closest parallels in the Egyptian, Semitic, and Sumerian traditions of wisdom poetry which together form a continuous tradition from 2500 B.C. to the early centuries of our era. There is plentiful archaeological evidence for growing Eastern influence on Greek culture throughout the eighth century B.C. Hesiod lived toward the end of that century, and whatever the channels by which this influence came, he seems to have been peculiarly well placed to benefit from it.

Hesiodic poetry is sometimes held to have been characteristic of Boeotia or of mainland Greece (simply because that is where Hesiod lived), and Homeric poetry of Ionia. In fact there is no reason to think that both types were not current in most parts of Greece. What is certain is that the epic language and style reached their definitive form in the Ionian area which stretched from Athens and Euboea in the west across the islands of the central Aegean to the coast of Asia Minor. In the course of the eighth century this brilliant Ionian tradition became more widely known, arousing in the Greeks of the mainland a new interest in and respect for the glories of the heroic past. Ancient graves began to be treated with a new reverence, to be attributed to particular heroes of legend, and to be brought offerings. Relics of Bronze Age buildings became the sites of new shrines. Heroic scenes appeared in art. Mainland poets such as Hesiod began to compose hexameter poetry in the Ionian manner and in the (predominantly) Ionian epic dialect. It is reasonable to suppose that Hesiod used this form for a genealogical poem and a wisdom poem because such poems already existed in the Ionian tradition.

VI

Where Homer stands in that tradition is a matter for controversy. To ascribe the eighth-century expansion of epic to his personal influence, as some have done, is to beg a very large question. *Iliad* and *Odyssey* — the colossal written poems which are the object of inquiry — presuppose an easier familiarity with writing than can readily be assumed so early. The writer of this chapter has always held that they belong in the seventh century. Not till the last quarter of that century is there solid evidence for the existence and fame of the *Iliad,* and some less solid evidence for the *Odyssey*.

But another hundred years, and Homer and Hesiod are established as the two great names in hexameter poetry. At Athens it is decided that every four years, at the Great Panathenaic festival, teams of rhapsodes will recite the *Iliad* and *Odyssey* entire, over a period of days; the division of each poem into twenty-four 'rhapsodies', that is 'recitations', which is certainly not original, may date from this time. Partial recitations were an everyday experience. Homer — in the sense of those two poems — became the basis of education. Throughout antiquity he remained the most widely read and influential of all Greek authors, often cited simply as 'the Poet', and acknowledged as unsurpassable, the great source from which all lesser streams flowed.

3   Other early poetry

I

The rest of early Greek poetry down to about 500 B.C. is sometimes loosely lumped together as 'lyric'. This is unfortunate, because it implies that that poetry had a unity which it did not have, and because the word 'lyric' has associations which are largely inappropriate. In an ancient context it properly refers to poetry sung or recited to the accompaniment of the lyre. But the rhapsodes who recited epic poetry at least sometimes accompanied themselves on the lyre; while much of the smaller-scale poetry to be reviewed in this chapter was accompanied by the pipes, or not at all. Often we do not know how it was performed.

It is better (though still not completely satisfactory) to divide it into melic poetry, iambic poetry, elegy, and epigram. Melic poetry means simply song, whether solo or choral, and naturally covers a very wide range. Iambic poetry, which sounds like a metrical category, in fact includes more than one kind of verse associated with the *iambos*, a particular sort of entertainment. Elegy is a purely metrical category, comprising verse composed in elegiac couplets; it has none of the mournful associations that the word carries in the context of English literature. Epigram, in this period, stands apart: it is verse not intended for oral delivery but to be written on a physical object as a label. Only later, when the verse inscription comes to be the subject of literary imitation, does it become a department of book literature.

Much of this poetry has survived only in fragments: quotations by later authors and remnants of ancient papyrus copies recovered from Egypt. Complete poems are rare until we come to Pindar in the fifth century. But enough survives for us to trace the main lines of development, and to appreciate the qualities of the principal poets and the justification for the reputations they enjoyed; enough to delight and tantalize us. The continuing publication of papyrus fragments is still adding materially to our knowledge of this area.

Since accounts of Greek literature so often treat epic and 'lyric' as successive stages in its development, the point must be made again that date of first appearance in writing is no reliable guide to date of origin. However old epic poetry may be, song is older. From time immemorial men sang as they brought in the harvest, women as they ground the corn, children in their play, choruses at festivals. Homer himself refers to the singing of paeans to propitiate Apollo in time of danger, harvest songs, and laments for the dead; Circe sings as she weaves. The study of comparative metrics has shown that it is in melic poetry, not epic, that the oldest forms of Greek verse are to be found — forms recognizably related to early Indian, Slavic, and other Indo-European verse forms, and thus going back by a continuous tradition to the remote times when these peoples were together. Epic for its part continued to be composed in the traditional style into the fifth century, that is, for two hundred years after melic and other kinds of poetry had begun to be written down.

By the time this poetry comes into sight, regional traditions have developed, differing from each other in metre, dialect, and probably musical style. But just as epic spread beyond the Ionian area where it reached perfection, so in time other regional styles spilled over local boundaries and were imitated more generally. They had grown too far apart for complete fusion, and they retained elements of their separate identities, particularly in respect of dialect. For example, elegy belonged with epic in the Ionian tradition, and throughout history it was normally composed with an Ionic dialect colouring, wherever the poet happened to come from. Similarly, poetry in the Doric manner is composed by Ionian and Athenian poets with a Doric dialect colouring. The dialect in which Greek literary works were composed always depended more on the genre to which it belonged than on the author's place of origin. The literary dialects were seldom identical with spoken dialects: they were subject to various influences, such as the native speech habits of the writer himself and of all his predecessors in the genre, and archaisms borrowed from the epic language.

The degree to which poetic language was removed from ordinary speech also varied according to genre. The main features which distinguished it before 500 B.C. were the use of old words and grammatical forms, the free addition of ornamental adjectives and adverbs, and the avoidance of words felt to be coarse or undignified. It is in epic that these features are most in evidence; elegy and melic poetry come next on the scale, then spoken iambic verse, some of which does approach the level of colloquial language. What is not characteristic of poetry at this period is any straining after novelty or originality of expression. Indeed, the use of ready-made phrases borrowed from others is almost an essential element in convincing poetic style. The poet's effort is not directed towards expanding the boundaries of art but towards organizing his thoughts and feelings for persuasive presentation; the poetic form in which he expresses them is something given, a familiar, comfortable vessel. Sometimes he achieves originality spontaneously, but he does not officiously strive for it. The result is that this poetry is consistently clear and straightforward; when it is obscure, it is usually because we are ignorant about something that was well known to the original audience, and not because the poet failed to express himself in a natural way.

In our own culture verse that is written to be set to music rarely gives much satisfaction when read on its own. The best poetry is to be found elsewhere. In ancient Greece the situation is quite different. Melody was not considered a substitute for substance. Much of the finest, most profound and most difficult poetry was designed to be sung. Of the music we have only the rhythms, mirrored in the precise, often complex metres of the verse, which repeat themselves from stanza to stanza or in the triadic pattern of strophe, antistrophe, epode, that is, two stanzas with the same melody, a third with a different one, and then the pattern repeated, AABAABAAB ... In the case of choral song there was often a further aspect to the performance: dancing. A chorus presupposes a definite ceremonial occasion and a sizeable audience. It might be a regular festival with religious associations, or some special event, an emergency supplication to the gods, a wedding or a funeral, a celebration of military or athletic victory. Where dancing was part of the procedure, it was commonly done by the singers. So in reading some texts, we have to bear in mind that they are only part of a whole. We must try to supply in imagination the music, the dancing, the atmosphere of the occasion.

II

There was one archaic poet whom the ancients considered worthy to be named beside Homer and Hesiod, despite much in his work that shocked their sensibilities. This was Archilochus, who flourished about 650. He was a native of Paros, just in the middle of the Aegean, but he spent part of his life on Thasos, a Parian colony off the Thracian coast. His poetry, elegiac and iambic, is concerned with the world about him, his reactions to contemporary events both public and private: politics, war, shipwrecks, personal affairs. There is a wide variety of tone, from grave to gay, from pleasantly bantering to bitter. He believed in the traditional rule of loving one's friends and hating one's enemies, and he seems to have made plenty of the latter. He prided himself on his ability to repay evil with evil. But he was capable of facing adversity with dignity:

> Heart, my heart, with helpless, sightless troubles now confounded,
>> up, resist the enemy, opposing breast to breast!
> All about they lie in wait, but stand thou firmly grounded,
>> not rudely proud in victory, nor in defeat oppressed.
> In thy rejoicing let thy joy, in hardship thy despairs
> be tempered. Understand the pattern shaping men's affairs.
>
> (Archilochus, fr 128)

In a less serious vein, we find him rebuking a friend who came uninvited to a party, made no contribution, and drank heavily; bidding the Muse to 'sing of Glaucus the quiff-moulder'; jesting about having had to abandon his shield in battle to save his life ('To the devil with it! I'll get another just as good'). This last piece was notorious in antiquity, and it has sometimes been held up as marking a reaction against Homeric values. More likely Archilochus was simply speaking as a soldier among his mates, who knew the reality of war. He was not attacking anyone's ideal or putting forward one of his own.

He may not always be speaking in his own person when he appears to be, for we know of two poems of his which began with speeches in the mouths of others without any immediate indication of the fact. Caution is particularly necessary in connection with the genus *iambos*. Archilochus is one of several Ionian poets who composed entertaining monologues and songs anciently classified as *iamboi* (the iambic metre was named after them) and apparently destined for certain merry carnivals associated with Demeter and Dionysus; Paros was one of the main centres of Demeter's cult. Comic raillery and a certain amount of obscenity were traditional on these occasions, and the outspoken sexuality, invective, and other vulgarities which we meet in iambic poets, and not in other poetry of the period, evidently reflect the special conventions of the festival or festivals concerned. In particular we find fragments of extravagant sexual narratives in the first person, accounts of licentious goings-on at which the speaker represented himself as having taken part. If convention required them, clearly they did not have to be true, and they have the air of fantasies. It is conceivable that the poets presented them in the guise of stock characters rather than in their own persons.

Archilochus repeatedly attacked in his *iamboi* one Lycambes, who had (at any rate according to later tradition) betrothed his daughter Neobule to him but later broken off the arrangement. The poet claimed to have had illicit relations with both Lycambes' daughters, and described their activities in such lurid detail that the family (so the story goes) hanged themselves for shame. A recently published papyrus, the longest continuous piece of Archilochus that survives, tells of an encounter between him and Neobule's younger sister in a lonely meadow. Much of it is taken up with reporting what they said to each other — he persuading her to lie with him, she trying to divert his interest to Neobule, whom he dismisses as overblown and promiscuous. At the end he describes how he gently pulled her down into the flowers, spread his cloak over them, caressed her breasts, and finally satisfied his desire, using coitus interruptus as he had promised. It is a strong, lively poem, full of feeling. The description of the sexual act, though explicit, avoids coarse, physical words, using metaphors instead: 'do not begrudge me to go under the coping-stone and the gates, for I will put ashore at the grassy gardens'; 'I discharged my [hot](?) strength'. This verbal delicacy is due to the melic nature of the piece: it does not extend to fragments from *iamboi* in spoken verse.

Another seventh-century iambographer, Semonides of Amorgos (not to be confused with the later melic poet Simonides), can also be seen to have composed narratives of that character, but the two surviving fragments of his verse that are of any length are much more decent. The main one is the so-called 'satire on women', 118 lines which almost constitute a complete poem. It propounds the thesis that different sorts of women were made from different animals, and get their qualities from them. In the sow-woman's house, for instance, everything lies in a mess on the floor, and she, unwashed and in dirty clothes, sits feeding herself fat amid the filth. In the whole series only the bee-woman is wholly praiseworthy; the rest have scarcely one good quality among them. Semonides concludes that women are a great nuisance, imposed on men by Zeus. This boorish and unwitty poem, in which each woman is mechanically constructed from the features of her animal, was meant to entertain a male audience that in general shared the poet's depreciatory attitude towards the female sex. A century later Hipponax wrote that 'two days in a woman's life give most pleasure — when she is married, and when she is buried'.

The fragments of Hipponax's *iamboi* are characterized by a picaresque vulgarity of language and substance that masks considerable poetic skill and sophistication. He assumes the role of a low buffoon, and a burglar:

> Hermes, dear Hermes, Maia's son, Cyllenian,
> hear thou my prayer, for I am frozen terrible,
> my teeth are chattering . . .
> Grant Hipponax a cloak and a nice tunic
> and some nice sandals and nice fur boots —
> and sixty gold staters by the other wall . . .
> For thou hast never granted me a cloak
> thick in the winter to cure me of the shivers,
> nor hast thou put my feet in thick fur boots
> to stop my chilblains bursting.
>   (Hipponax, frr 32, 34)

The combination of solemn form and banal content is deliberately comic, much as in Belloc's sonnet 'Would that I had £300,000'. So is Hipponax's use of grotesque compound words: 'shoulder-deep-gawping Mimnes', 'in-mid-meal-shitter'. His reported sexual adventures are sordid and farcical. In one fragmentary payprus he is treated for impotence by a witch, who uses a combination of spells, anal stimulants, and flagellation, with dubious results:

> She spoke in Lydian: *'Faskat ikrol'l'* —
> in Arsish, 'Up the arse [',]
> and [pulling down] my ball by the bal[d patch]
> she thrashed me with a fig-branch, like [a scapegoat]
> fast[ened in] the stocks. And there [I was]
> under two torments: on one side the branch
> [was killing] me, descending from above,
> [my arse on the other] spattering me with shit.
> The passage stank; and dung-beetles came buzzing
> after the smell, over fifty of them:
> some attacked, while others [whet] their te[eth],
> and others fell upon the Arsenal doors . . .

> (Hipponax, fr 92)

III

From *iambos* we return to the more decorous Ionian form of elegy. The two other elegists of Archilochus' generation, Callinus of Ephesus and Tyrtaeus of Sparta, although living on opposite sides of the Aegean, write remarkably similar poetry, both exhorting their fellow-citizens to win glory in the defence of their country. Callinus' audience seems to be unprepared for war, perhaps enjoying their symposium; Tyrtaeus, however, speaks to men already drawn up for battle. The idea of an army, about to fight, pausing to listen to a poet may strike us as strange; but it is attested that in the fourth century B.C., when Tyrtaeus was an established classic, the Spartans when under arms were made to assemble before the king's quarters to listen to recitations from his work. He seems to have been something of a state poet, perhaps a retainer of the two Spartan kings. At a time when civil discord threatened their authority and that of the council of elders, Tyrtaeus composed a propaganda poem, known to later writers as *Eunomia*, 'Law and Order', which called for obedience to the rulers and an end to strife.

The use of elegy to arouse martial enthusiasm and courage continued to the end of the seventh century, being found in Mimnermus of Smyrna and Solon of Athens. These poets,

however, are better remembered for other things. Mimnermus
was famous for poetry celebrating the pleasures of love and
youth. The more personal parts of it are lost, but we have a few
precious excerpts containing general reflections on the subject.
Here is one of the longest:

> What then is life? Where is pleasure, without Aphrodite the golden?
>   Die may I rather, before such things delight me no more!
> Friendship's secret joys, and honeysweet gifts and the love-bed —
>   Such in our youth are the flowers (pluck if we will) that are ours,
> Both men and women. But when old age with its pains comes upon
>   us,
>   Age, destroying a man, leaves him dishonour and shame;
> Ever his mind is beset, worn down by his trouble and weakness;
>   Even the bright sun's rays cannot give joy to his eyes.
> Then he's repulsive to boys, and women no longer admire him.
>   Age is a toil and a curse, sent by the hard will of Zeus.
>
>   (Mimnermus fr 1, translation A. N. Palmer)

Sunlight is a favourite theme of Mimnermus', almost an obses-
sion. So is the contrast between the brief joy of youth and the
horrors of old age, worse than death itself.

We know Solon above all as a statesman, and some of his
poetry is political. But his elegies also allow us to see a more
private side. He shared Mimnermus' hedonism, and wrote that
bodily comforts, the possession of a beautiful boy or woman, are
wealth just as truly as gold, silver and estates; you cannot take it
with you when you die, or buy off illness, old age, or death. But he
criticized Mimnermus for having prayed for a painless death at
sixty, telling him he ought to substitute 'eighty'. This is the first
known instance of one Greek author explicitly referring to
another.

Solon's political poetry was a major source for later historians,
and our picture of his achievements as a statesman is based
ultimately upon it. There is accordingly a danger of taking him
too much at his own assessment. Like Tyrtaeus, he lectures his
fellow-citizens on the importance of law and order, warning them
against giving power to demagogues. After being given special
legislative powers himself, he defends his actions against critics,
in iambic rhythms and rhetoric that blazes with pride and
righteousness.

I call as witness in the court of Time
the mighty mother of the Olympian gods,
dark Earth, from whom I lifted boundary-stones
that did beset her — slave before, now free.
And many to Athena's holy land
I brought back, sold abroad illegally
or legally, and others whom their debts
had forced to leave, their speech no longer Attic,
so great their wanderings; and others here
in ugly serfdom at their masters' mercy
I set free. These things I did in power,
blending strength with justice, carried out
all that I promised. I wrote laws for all,
for high and low alike, made straight and just.

(Solon, fr 36.3–20)

Solon is one of the most forceful and imaginative of the elegiac poets. Vivid metaphors and similes spring readily to his mind. Obedience to law, he says, 'makes the rough smooth, ends excess, dims violence, and withers the growing flowers of ruin'. The punishment of Zeus falls on the sinner like a sudden wind that drives away the clouds and makes the sky bright again.

The largest body of archaic elegiac verse that remains to us is a collection of poems and excerpts, some 1400 lines in all, preserved under the name of the Megarian Theognis. Theognis is actually only one poet among many represented; there are bits of Tyrtaeus, Solon, and others, and the greater part must be regarded as anonymous elegy from between the seventh and the fifth century. Besides political and moralizing verse — much of it marked as Theognis' by his habit of addressing his friend Cyrnus — we find a good deal of more genial and personal character. Many of the pieces were composed to be sung at the symposium with accompaniment from a piper. Often they are on the subject of drinking or making merry, and there are some charming things among them.

I'm heavy-headed with wine, Onomacritus, not any longer
in control of my mind; drink has me on the retreat.
Here is the room going round and round. I'd better try standing,
find out whether the wine's also got hold of my legs
and of my innermost wits. I'm afraid I'll do something silly
in my fortified state, badly disgracing myself. (*Theognidea* 503–8)

Other poems are reflective or philosophic, and develop an argument on some ethical or practical question, for example whether it is better to spend freely and enjoy life, running the risk of bankruptcy, or to be parsimonious, and risk leaving one's fortune to someone else. The last 150 lines of the collection are devoted to love poems, mostly to unnamed boys, pleading for their favours in decorous phrases like 'hear my prayer', 'do not be unfair to me', or reproaching them with infidelity. Many of them are conventional and banal, but one or two are touching.

> Lad, your reckless behaviour destroyed my sensible instincts,
>   and our friends were ashamed, knowing about the affair:
> But for a little while you cooled my fever; my speeding
>   voyage into the night briefly found haven from storm.
>
> (*Theognidea* 1271–4)

Such pieces might no doubt be borrowed by many different men for their own use.

IV

The predominantly paederastic orientation of archaic love poetry was of course the consequence of social factors. The men and boys talked and drank and went about together; slave girls, musicians and the like, were to hand, but wives and daughters played little part in social life. From the melic poetry of Sappho, however, we see that in the Aeolic island of Lesbos, at least, about 600 B.C., there was a women's society which was the mirror image of the men's, with their own symposia and love affairs. It appears to have been a group of unmarried women or girls, who gathered in Sappho's house to practise music and song and at other times sang in public at weddings and festivals. Some of Sappho's fragments are from such public songs, but most are from songs composed for their private gatherings and concerned with personal matters. Almost all are in short, simple stanzas of two, three, or four lines. Thought and language also tend to be simple, even commonplace; yet simplicity is sometimes the best vehicle of intensity. There is nothing commonplace about her tribute to a departed friend who, she sings, shines now among the women of Lydia like the moon among the stars, shedding its light on the sea and the flowery fields, with a fair dew that nourishes the roses, the soft chervil and the honey-clover. We are given the impression of a young woman who is not only beautiful but sheds a life-giving radiance upon those around her.

The one complete poem that we have exemplifies one of the commonest themes of ancient love poetry: 'Oh dear, I am in love *again*.' It is cast in the form of a prayer to Aphrodite, and built round an ornate, fanciful description of previous visits which the goddess has paid to Sappho, flying down in a car drawn by sparrows. It is one of several of her songs which achieve a neat rounded form by echoing the beginning at the end. We know of nothing earlier in world literature that has a beginning, middle and end so clearly marked out. Here is another example, which is a better illustration than the prayer poem of Sappho's simple style:

> Some think a fleet, a troop of horse
> or soldiery the finest sight
> in all the world; but I say, what one loves.
>
> Easy it is to make this plain
> to anyone. She the most fair
> of mortals, Helen, having a man of the best,
>
> Deserted him, and sailed to Troy,
> without a thought for her dear child
> or parents, led astray by [love's power.]
>
> [For though the heart be pr]oud [and strong,]
> [Love] quickly [bends it to his will.—]
> That makes me think of Anactoria.
>
> I'd sooner see her lovely walk
> and the bright sparkling of her face
> than all the horse and arms of Lydia.

(Sappho, fr 16)

Alcaeus lived in the same town of Mytilene at the same time as Sappho, and yet there is hardly one certain sign of contact between them. He inhabits the man's world. His love poems were about boys, his drinking songs for male comrades, his other interests mainly political. Like many other towns in the seventh and sixth centuries, Mytilene was going through a period of instability, with revolutions and dictatorships. Alcaeus belonged to a prominent land-owning family, and, in intrigue with others of his class, he opposed the dictators; but the town was not in sympathy with him, and he was exiled. He probably sang his political songs to his cronies at supper. Here they are in danger from one of the dictators, Myrsilus:

> This wave looks higher than the first:
> we'll have a job to bale it out
> if once it comes aboard [...
>
> *
>
> Let's quickly batten down and run for port.
>
> Let none be soft or slow to move:
> we all can see the [trials] ahead.
> Remember last time! Every man be brave,
>
> And let us not disgrace [...]
> our worthy fathers in their graves,
> who [...] this town...
>
> (Alcaeus, fr 6. 1–16)

In one song Alcaeus calls for deep drinking as the best response to setbacks; in another, to celebrate Myrsilus' death. Any occasion is justification enough for drinking: the presence of winter, or spring, or summer, or the simple reflection that man is mortal and will not see the sun again once he dies. Alcaeus seems to have been an uncomplicated man, and his poetry, though vigorous and memorable, has no special brilliance or subtlety. Most people would prefer the next new papyrus of Aeolic lyric to be of Sappho.

V

From about the same period, or a trifle earlier, we get our first extensive specimen of choral poetry, in the Partheneion (girls' song) of Alcman, who was active in Sparta a generation or so after Tyrtaeus. Although all Greece knew choral song of some sort, it seems to have been highly developed only in the Dorian sphere, and Doric became the conventional dialect colouring for it. A feature of the Dorian tradition was the construction of much longer and more varied strophes than we find in Ionian or Aeolian song. Thus Alcman's Partheneion is in strophes of fourteen lines; later poets will make their lines longer and rhythmically more complex. The song is a festival piece for a chorus of ten girls, who sing and dance at a religious ceremony of uncertain nature. The opening is lost. The earlier part of the surviving text alternates between moralizing and myth, in a way typical of lyric poetry: a general truth leads to a mythical illustration (the story being told more or less sketchily), and from there the poet passes back to his starting-point, or to a new generalization. The last sixty lines of the Partheneion are occupied with personal matters, especially the beauty of two girls who are attending to a sacrifice. There is a suggestion that one of them arouses erotic desires in other girls. This seems to have been a conventional element, for it appears also in some beautiful but tantalizing fragments from another of Alcman's Partheneia. Its relevance to the festival is one of many points that remain unclear about both poems, despite the apparent simplicity of their language. But more than anything else in archaic poetry, they seem like windows into a lost world.

It was long supposed that Stesichorus wrote for a chorus, but this now appears unlikely. He was active in Sicily, Italy, and probably Sparta sometime in the mid-sixth century, and left a considerable number of lyric poems, remarkable for the large scale on which they were composed, the line-count running into the thousands. They were in effect epics, in subject as well as in length, only to be sung to broadly-drawn melodies on the triadic system instead of chanted to Homer's single repeating verse. They must have taken well over an hour to perform. The musical effect must have been somewhat monotonous, for in at least one poem the melody of the initial strophe recurred more than a hundred times. As a natural corollary of his predominantly dactylic metres, epic subject-matter, and narrative amplitude, Stesichorus' style is more Homeric than lyric poetry usually is, with many formulaic epithets, long speeches, similes, etc., but also some colourful touches of his own. In one piece we find him following a passage of the *Odyssey* quite closely, and elsewhere he may be using lost epics in a similar way. We should be able to appreciate him better if we were in a position to read him in long, continuous stretches. This is not yet possible, though recent discoveries have given us a much clearer picture than we had. His themes included several of Heracles' adventures, the Trojan War and the returns of the Greek heroes, Orestes' avenging of his father, the story of Oedipus' sons, and other legends of central Greece. He was important as a source for the tragedians.

The poet who sought fame beyond his own circle or reward for his efforts had to seek patronage, either from the general public, gathered at festivals or market, or from some wealthy family. At intervals in Greek history potentates appeared whose interest in poets was great enough to attract them from far afield. In the second half of the sixth century two Samian rulers fulfil this role, Aeaces and his son Polycrates, and after them Hipparchus at Athens; it may have been Hipparchus who organized the recitation of Homer at the Great Panathenaea. To Samos came Ibycus from Rhegium in south Italy and Anacreon from the Ionian colony of Abdera in Thrace. It is interesting to compare the two. In dialect and metre they stand apart, for Ibycus belongs to the Dorian tradition, with special affinities to his fellow westerner Stesichorus, while Anacreon writes in his native Ionic and in Ionian and Aeolian rhythms. Both make similar use of the 'in love again' theme, with vivid imagery for the onset of love. Both represent the god Eros as a tempter, trying to induce the poet to involve himself. But whereas Ibycus will spring from one metaphor to another, with chaotic overall effect, Anacreon is capable of sustaining and developing a single image, as in this wry song to a Thracian girl:

> Thracian filly, why so sharply
> shy away with sidelong glances,
>   thinking I've no expertise?
>
> Be assured, I'd put your bit on
> smartly, hold the reins and run you
>   round the limits of the course.
>
> But for now you graze the meadows,
> frisk and play, for want of any
>   good experienced riding man.
>   (Anacreon, *PMG** 417)

Anacreon has other themes besides love: drinking and making merry, satirical comment on personalities, occasionally death.

*PMG = Poetae Melici Graei ed. D. L. Page (Oxford, 1962).

But everywhere he shows the same perfection of form, the ability to match the structure and emphasis of this thought to that of the verse, with each word as functional as a jewel in a Swiss watch. In him the archaic style reaches a brilliant culmination.

After the fall of Polycrates he moved on to Athens, where among Hipparchus' protégés he must have met Simonides of Ceos. Here if anywhere we can say that archaic met classical. By 'classical' in this antithesis we must understand not the cool and severe and all that is evoked by classical temples and statues that have lost their paint, but on the contrary something more garish, more rococo. For what nearly all types of poetry have in common in the fifth century — hexameters, elegy, lyric, tragedy — is a new tendency to complexity and artificiality of thought and diction. It is less spontaneous, more intellectual, more difficult. Simonides was nearly sixty at the turn of the century, and not affected by the change to the same extent as younger men. But it was not unconnected with the emergence of a new sort of professionalism, of which he was the prime exponent. He traded openly on his reputation — his avarice was notorious — and found patrons in many parts of Greece as well as in Sicily and Italy. They were paying for a more than ordinary ability to manipulate language and contrive music.

Simonides became a Panhellenic poet in another sense too. The Persian wars gave Greece a new consciousness of national identity. Simonides celebrated the great battles in elegy, epigram, and song. The spectacle of Xerxes' defeat tremendously reinforced the traditional conviction that pride goes before a fall, and that human prosperity, however well grounded it may appear, is at the mercy of the gods. This is a theme dear to Simonides, who was given to moralizing and the discussion of ethical questions. Sometimes he took a famous saying as a text for criticism or argument, as in the song where he cited the epitaph of Midas ascribed to Cleobulus, tyrant of Lindos. The epitaph said that the memorial would stand as long as rivers flow, trees grow, the sun and moon rise. But (Simonides protests):

> Who of sound mind could assent to that Lindian, Cleobulus,
> who against ever-flowing rivers and flowers of spring,
> sun's flame, moon's gold and swirling sea

set the strength of — a memorial?
All things yield to the gods: a stone
even man's arts can shatter. This is the thought of a fool.

(Simonides, *PMG* 581)

The poetic images in this were supplied by the epitaph, and some
of Simonides' other disputations are somewhat lacking in them;
later in the fifth century such topics will become more the
province of sophists and prose writers. Yet one fragment suffices
to defend Simonides against the suspicion of prosiness: a marvellous description of Danae, adrift at sea in a chest with her baby
Perseus, and a storm brewing.

Oh, child! What trouble is mine, and you can sleep,
innocent heart, slumbering on comfortless
timber riveted with bronze, in black
darkness of unlit night.
The passing wave's spray upon your hair
disturbs you not, or the wind's noise,
as you lie in your royal cloth. Gentle face,
if fear were fear to you,
even my words would draw your tiny ear.
Yes, sleep, baby; and sleep, sea! Sleep, horror!
O father Zeus,
grant some sign of a change of thy will —
forgive me if I ask too much.

(Simonides *PMG* 543)

In his old age Simonides had competition from his nephew
Bacchylides and from the arrogant Theban, Pindar. All three
enjoyed the patronage of (among others) Hieron of Syracuse, who
made Sicily the cultural centre of Greece between 478 and 467.
Of the work of Pindar and Bacchylides we have a substantial
amount, but in both cases, as it happens, predominantly from
their Epinicia, choral odes celebrating sporting victories. They
also wrote hymns, paeans, partheneia, convivial songs, and other
pieces. Pindar is the greater of the two; also the more uneven and
the more difficult. The difficulty lies in his originality (even
eccentricity) of metaphor and involution of thought and phras-
ing. The involution may be illustrated from the ode composed for
Hieron's victory in the Olympic horse-race in 476. Pindar decides

to make a start by saying that the Olympic games are the greatest of all games. By the time he has wrapped up this simple idea a little, it has become 'water is supreme among liquids; gold is supreme among material possessions; and the Olympics are outstanding among games'. But he is not content with that. What actually comes out is:

> Supreme is water; gold shines
> like a burning fire in the night above all proud wealth;
> but if games are what thou yearnest to sing, my heart,
> seek not, after the sun, another luminary
> through the airy void with greater heat in the day,
> nor shall we call any contest superior to Olympia.
>
> (Pindar, *Olympian Odes* 1.1–7)

An untidy little paragraph; but without saying anything extravagant about the games, Pindar has succeeded in investing them with the splendour of water, gold, fire, and the sun.

The athletic record of the victor and his family provides further material, and here involution may become a necessity if the facts are to be accommodated at all compactly in the strict, complex metrical scheme.

> He is tasting contests;
> and to the Amphictionic
> host the Parnassian hollow has proclaimed him
> highest of boys in the circuit race.
> Apollo, sweet men's goal
> and their beginning grows when a god gives speed:
> he must have accomplished this
> by your design; but kinship walks in the steps
> of his father, Olympic victor twice
> in battle-bearing arms of Ares; also
> the deep-meadow contest under the cliffs of Cirrha
> made Phricias master-foot.
>
> (Pindar, *Pythian Odes* 10.7–16)

No archaic poet could have written in this contorted way.

Pindar is not much interested in sport for its own sake. The significance of the victory for him is that it manifests the innate quality of the man and his family. The bulk of most odes is taken up by moralizing and myths, as in other kinds of choral poetry.

Any myth can be used, and on the slightest pretext. It may have some connection with the victor's ancestry, or his home town, or the games at which he has been successful; it may have no particular relevance, its presence being ostensibly justified as an illustration of some commonplace such as 'there is a time and place for everything'. Pindar's attitude to myth is flexible. He is prepared to adapt it to suit his patrons or his own moral sense. He was not exceptional in this; the Greeks never regarded tradition as sacrosanct, but as raw material for the artist's use.

He does not follow any fixed pattern in constructing an ode, and one is often left with the impression of a suitcase filled rather at random. Yet there are odes which impress as architecture and are thoroughly integrated wholes. Foremost among them is Pindar's masterpiece, the first Pythian ode. It is worth giving a brief account of this poem, as an indication of what Pindar at his most inspired was able to make out of the epinician form.

It was composed in 470 for Hieron on the occasion of a chariot victory; it was at the same time a celebration of the new town of Etna, which Hieron had founded below the volcano and put in the charge of his son Deinomenes, and of the battle of Cumae in 474, at which he had broken the Etruscan sea power. It is in five triads, Pindar's normal maximum: just a hundred lines as conventionally divided. The first strophe and antistrophe present a wonderful vision of Apollo playing the lyre in heaven for the chorus of Muses. The gods are at peace, Zeus' fiery thunderbolt flickers out, his great eagle is lulled to sleep by the divine music, even Ares, disarmed, drowses contentedly. The epode, with its change of tune, brings a contrast: Zeus' enemies are bewildered by the distant sound of the Muses' song, and especially the many-headed monster Typhon, firmly and painfully confined under the cliffs of Cumae and under Etna. Although it is not said in so many words, Typhon clearly symbolized Hieron's defeated enemies, and the divine concert his present leisure. From Typhon Pindar passes straight to the new town, whose protecting god Zeus is, and to Hieron's athletic victory. In the course of the third triad he recalls Hieron's battles, and his ill health; the myth of Philoctetes comes in briefly as a neat and complimentary parallel. Then he moves on to Deinomenes, with the justification that 'the father's victory is no alien rejoicing to him'. He prays to Zeus that

Etna may continue as it has begun, referring explicitly now to the Etruscan calamity at Cumae and his own role as the poet who celebrates Greek victories over barbarians. This state of affairs in the world of men mirrors the divine situation described in the first triad. The final triad consists of admonitions for the young king, and a reference at the end to the lyres that resound for successful rulers takes us back to the start.

Bacchylides' poetry is less demanding than Pindar's, his thought, language, and construction more predictable. The touch of genius is lacking; and yet his songs must have been very agreeable to listen to. The most remarkable among them, because we know nothing else like it, is not a victory ode but a short dramatization of a scene from legend, with alternate strophes in the mouth of Aegeus, king of Athens, and a chorus representing his subjects. The theme is the young, unknown Theseus, Aegeus' son, who has grown to manhood at Trozen and is now on his way to the city from the Isthmus; the song portrays the tension that his approach creates. As in Attic tragedy, what is shown is not so much a mythical event itself as people's feelings and reactions towards it. Possibly the song is the last survival from a tradition akin to that from which Attic drama developed; alternatively it may itself have been inspired by the Athenian model.

Towards the end of the fifth century Greek music underwent something of a revolution. A new, freer sort of melody developed which was not bound by the constraint of repetition in strophe and antistrophe but could adapt itself continually to the sense and overtones of the words, and so contribute to the expression of character and mood. Aristophanes parodies Euripides' indulgence, in his last years, in solo arias in the new style, and his setting of the word 'whirling' on a trill or shake. One of the leaders of this movement was the Milesian Timotheus, who composed choral narratives for pipe accompaniment and others that he sang solo to the lyre. In a sense he is a successor to Stesichorus, but with a very different manner. We have the last 240 lines of his *Persians,* which, like Aeschylus' play of the same name, dealt with the battle of Salamis. The language is elaborate, exuberant, highly coloured; Timotheus has a genuine gift of imagination and a sense of dramatic realism, but also a lack of taste which leads him close to absurdity.

> The emerald-haired sea was furrowed red
> from naval oozings; confused shouting prevailed,
> while the barbarian naval host
> was swept back in a mass on the fish-wreathed
> gleamfold bosom of Amphitrite . . .

> From their hands they dropped the mountain feet of the ship
>   [i.e. oars made from pine or fir]
> and from their mouth leapt forth
> its gleamshine children all in a clatter [i.e. their teeth].
>   (Timotheus, *PMG* 791 31–9; 90–3)

In a later passage an Asiatic captive is represented pleading with his captor in a peculiar broken Greek. This type of realism, imitation of foreigners' speech, is earlier found only in comedy for humorous purposes. There is nothing of the kind with Aeschylus' Persians, for example, or Homer's Trojans. In an epilogue Timotheus defends his novelties against critics, saying that music has always been a developing art, and that he stands in a succession of great innovators that goes back to Orpheus. His poetic style had no lasting influence; his music did.

VI

The most important of the elegiac, iambic, and melic poets have now been mentioned. It remains to say a brief word about the epigram, the verse inscription. We have one or two examples from as early as the late eighth century, but they do not become numerous till the sixth. The two main categories are epitaphs and dedications. Their authors, often ordinary people of no great poetic attainment, show little ambition in this earlier period to do more than convey essential information, and they seldom exceed four lines. In the epitaphs, however, we do find by the second half of the sixth century — at least in Athens — some attempts to arouse the sympathy of the passer-by as well as merely informing him.

> O you who go on your way with your mind on other engagements,
>   stop and feel sorrow beside Thrason's memorial here.
>   (Anon. (Hansen) no.31)

This is the tomb of a boy: be sorrowful as you behold it:
  Smicythus' death has bereft nearest and dearest of hope.
                                        ((Hansen) no.58)

After the Persian wars we find some longer and more rhetorical epitaphs, especially in publicly commissioned war memorials. This one commemorates the Athenians who fell on Cimon's Cyprian campaign in 449/8:

Never since Europe and Asia in twain by sea were divided,
  while wild Ares has been haunting the cities of man,
has there a finer deed been wrought by men under heaven
  all at one and the same moment at sea and on land.
These men slaughtered the Medes in Cyprus in plentiful numbers.
  and a Phoenician fleet, fivescore of ships on the main
crowded with men they took; and Asia loudly lamented
  under the blows that with both hands they had dealt them in war.
                                ([Simonides], epigram 45 (D. L. Page))

This is one of a large number of epigrams ascribed in literary tradition to Simonides — in this case anachronistically. Such ascriptions are generally meaningless. There is good evidence for Simonides' authorship in the case of one epitaph for a friend of his at Thermopylae, but in principle verse inscriptions are anonymous. Only in the fourth century did they begin to be treated as of literary interest, collected in books, and attributed wholesale to particular poets. With that, the way was open for the composition of purely literary epigrams, a development which will be followed in a later chapter.

4 Tragedy

I

If a reciter of epic comes before us at a festival and intones

> Then arose the hero, the son of Atreus, ruler of wide
> domains, Agamemnon,
>   wrathful, and all his heart was deeply darkened and
> filled with anger, and his eyes were like the flickering
> of fire,
>   and he spoke first to Calchas, with evil in his look:
> 'Prophet of woe, never yet have you foretold me weal . . .'
>   (Homer, *Iliad* i 101–6)

we may compliment him by calling his performance 'dramatic', if he utters it with pathos and conviction, but he is none the less a narrator of a story. If, on the other hand, he comes before us and begins straightway

> 'Prophet of woe, never yet have you foretold me weal . . .'

he is an actor, and this is drama. He is, so to speak, being Agamemnon, no longer simply telling us what Agamemnon said, and it is still drama even if he is wearing everyday clothes and even if Calchas is invisible to us. Exactly when and in what circumstances a Greek poet took the crucial step of composing for an actor, we do not know. It may well be that humorous performances, in which individuals or a chorus dressed up as if they were satyrs or foreigners or old women, are of immemorial antiquity, and the birth of tragedy was simply the application of this technique to serious matter. Tragedy was an Athenian invention, and by 500 B.C. its presentation was established as a part of one of the annual festivals in honour of the god Dionysus, the City Dionysia, celebrated in spring.

This was the beginning of serious drama in the western world. Yet its flowering and fading as an art-form were practically encompassed by one century, the fifth century B.C., and the three poets represented by the tragedies which survive today were recognized by the Athenians of the next century as having achieved a 'classic' status which set them apart from their contemporaries and successors. These three are Aeschylus, who produced his first plays about 490 B.C. and died in 456; Sophocles, who first produced in 468 and continued with unabated artistic and intellectual vigour until his death at the end of 406 (his *Oedipus at Colonus* was produced posthumously); and Euripides, whose career runs from 455 until his death, at the court of the king of Macedon, early in 406 (his last plays, too, were posthumously produced, *Bacchae* being one of them). Many other tragic poets are known to us by name and citations, particularly Agathon, who enjoyed considerable success in the period 420–10 before opting for Macedonian royal patronage, but in the course of the fourth century new work was gradually edged out in favour of revivals of fifth-century masterpieces

From about the middle of the fifth century plays were produced at the Lenaea, a winter festival of Dionysus, as well as at the City Dionysia, and by the fourth they were produced also at festivals in parts of Attica other than the city of Athens — by which time, too, the taste for Attic tragedy had spread throughout the Greek world. The playwrights competed for prizes at the festivals, for the Greeks tended to think that if artists, like athletes, hunger for honour and fear the humiliation of defeat, the incompetent will be discouraged, the competent will do their utmost, and the community as a whole will benefit accordingly. At the City Dionysia each tragic poet was required to put on a 'tetralogy', that is, a set of three tragedies plus a fourth play of more frivolous character involving a chorus dressed as satyrs (Euripides broke with this tradition by putting on *Alcestis* instead of a satyr-play in 438). He could, if he wished, choose as the themes of his three tragedies three successive stages of the same story, so that the resulting 'trilogy' resembled the 'acts' of one gigantic drama. Aeschylus liked to do that, and his *Oresteia,* consisting of *Agamemnon, Choephori* ('Libation-bearers'), and *Eumenides,* is the one such trilogy surviving; it was more usual to put on a set of tragedies which had nothing to do with each other. The text of a Greek tragedy is short, sometimes performable in an hour and a quarter; but since we know nothing of the acting style and the pace of singing, we cannot tell how long it actually took to perform.

Plays were performed in the open air and in daylight. If the action was to be thought of as taking place in the dark, the words of the play had to make that plain, and the audience's imagination co-operated. For all practical purposes there was no way of playing an indoor scene (the theatre had no curtain), so that the poets tended to construct action which could plausibly be thought of as taking place out of doors; and when the revelation of an interior scene was unavoidable, it could be effected only by rolling out a low trolley, which, so to speak, brought the interior outside.

All Greek communities had always celebrated festivals with choral song and dance, and the earliest tragedy extended this traditional form to include an actor able to engage in dialogue (in spoken verse) with the chorus-leader. A second actor was added early in the fifth century, and a third in the 460s. The actors wore masks, and the same actor could be required (as sometimes in modern repertory) to take more than one part in the course of a play; thus there was no limit to the number of characters a poet could put into a play, but a serious restriction on how many of them he could bring on stage to speak in the same scene. The original creation of tragedy from choral song and dance was of the greatest importance for its subsequent development and character, for every tragedy had a chorus. When a playwright offered a set of plays to the official in charge of the festival, he was said to 'ask for a chorus'. The action of the play is broken into separate scenes by choral songs, during which the actors are as a rule off-stage, but there are also scenes in which one or more actors sing in dialogue or in alternation with the chorus. Thus the element of music and dance is far greater in a Greek play than in serious modern drama.

Choral lyric, like epic, had always taken as its predominant themes myths of the heroic age (what we would call the Late Bronze Age). Tragedy inherited and maintained this tradition. The tragic poet was certainly free to choose a more topical subject; Aeschylus' *Persians* in fact portrayed the lamentable homecoming of Xerxes, king of Persia, in whose defeat Aeschylus' audience had played a major part only eight years earlier (480), and in the 490s Phrynichus had made an ill-received tragedy out of the Persian capture of Miletus. This early experimentation, however, was not enduring, nor did public taste encourage the poet to make up characters and a plot which did not purport to be the re-enactment of a momentous past event. Hence the same titles recur throughout the history of tragedy: Aeschylus, Sophocles, Euripides, and Philocles in the fifth century, Achaeus, Antiphon, and Theodectes in the fourth, all wrote a *Philoctetes,* and Euripides and Astydamas, as well as Sophocles, wrote an *Antigone.*

The regular use of myth precludes a 'surprise ending' in the modern sense. If the Athenian audience knew anything of myth — and all of them knew something of it — they knew that Orestes killed Aegisthus and not Aegisthus Orestes. However, the stock of myth on which the dramatist could draw was very large; local variants of the same myth were numerous, and since no version of any myth had ever been accorded the status of revealed truth (the Greeks were fundamentally sceptical about the possibility of knowing the past for certain) every poet modified what he handled, by selection, interpretation, and invention. These processes, including creative invention, were not the product of a new sophistication at a late stage of Greek culture, but built into the transmission of myth from the beginning. In the archaic period, for example, the lyric poet Stesichorus created the story that the Helen who went to Troy with Paris was a phantom devised by the gods, the real Helen remaining chastely in Egypt while the Trojan War was fought. Euripides uses the Stesichorean myth in his *Helen,* but in his *Trojan Women* and *Orestes* he uses the older myth according to which Helen at Troy was the one and only Helen. In such circumstances it is unprofitable to ask 'Well, did Euripides believe that Helen went to Troy, or didn't he?'

The extent to which the dramatists could exercise their freedom within the framework of a single well-known myth is neatly illustrated by Aeschylus' *Choephori,* Sophocles' *Electra,* and Euripides' *Electra,* all of which portray the homecoming of Orestes, son of Agamemnon and Clytaemnestra, and his killing of his mother and her lover Aegisthus, with the help of his sister Electra. This is the only case in which three different poets' treatment of the same myth has survived. The three Electras are

alike in devotion to their father's memory and refusal of reconciliation with their mother, but they differ in temperament and
intensity of resolve. The three presentations of Orestes differ
similarly: the emphasis in his motivation is different, and so is his
future, foreshadowed at the end of each play. Sophocles' Orestes
will resume his rights as monarch with a good conscience,
whereas Aeschylus' and Euripides' Orestes will be pursued by
Furies. This is a bald statement of the differences and similarities
which are most easily described in a few words and most easily
assigned to one aspect or another of the myth as it was treated by
poets, painters, and sculptors of the pre-dramatic period, the
inheritance available to the dramatists. The more important
differences between the three tragic poets lie in the feelings which
they evoke on the subject of the relations between a brother, a
sister, their murdered father, their guilty mother, and a divine
command that their father be avenged.

Not many of us have occasion to avenge our fathers by killing
our adulterous mothers; fewer still unwittingly kill their fathers
and (equally unwittingly) marry their mothers, as Oedipus did
through ignorance of his own parentage. We do not nowadays
receive grotesque prophecies or appalling commands from ora-
cles or converse with deities appearing suddenly in human shape
or descending in radiance from the sky. Those inclined to
conclude from these facts that Greek tragedy is not about people
and that it therefore has nothing to say to us are recommended to
suspend judgment until they have read (or better, seen) a Greek
tragedy and have reflected on it. Different religions may be
irreconcilable when they are translated into sets of theological
propositions, but there is a sense also in which they are different
languages available for the description of the same experiences
and passions. Hatred of our parents or our children, lust for
revenge on a brother, self-destruction in preference to suffering
the humiliation of irremediable injustice, are all recurrent phenomena in human history; their nature as experiences transcends
the centuries, and so does their expression by a playwright who
knows what he is about, however diverse their occasions and
however alien to us the theatrical conventions in which they are
presented.

If it was expected that a playwright should choose a particular myth for dramatic treatment in order to illuminate a social or political problem which preoccupied the community at the time, we have to admit that no Greek ever alludes to such an expectation, and that in the case of the great majority of extant tragedies we could not even take the first step towards identifying the contemporary issues to which (on this hypothesis) they were relevant. The *Oresteia* is in some particulars an exception, to the extent that Aeschylus locates the palace of Agamemnon at Argos (not Mycenae), attributes the foundation of the Areopagus (the Athenian court which tried cases of wilful homicide) to the occasion of Orestes' trial for matricide, and introduces three separate references to eternal alliance between Athens and Argos — all of which is explicable in terms of events of the last few years before the production of the *Oresteia*. There are moments in other plays at which we can argue reasonably for the hypothesis that such-and-such events probably came into the minds of many members of the audience; but we cannot expect to determine through any relationship with known historical issues or events the dates of plays, such as Sophocles' *Ajax* or *Women of Trachis,* on which we have no independent evidence.

Dramatic festivals, like all Greek festivals, were held in honour of gods, and included processions and sacrifices. To that extent drama was religious, but to call a Greek play a 'religious ceremony' is misleading if 'religious' and 'ceremony' are given Christian connotations. The essence of a festival was to conciliate a deity by honouring and entertaining him as one would a noble human guest. The underlying assumption was that deities took the same pleasure as we do not only in being the beneficiaries of effort and expense on the part of others but also in poetry, song, music, dance, laughter, colour, and jewellery, not to mention (though deities differed in character, and not everything was appropriate to every occasion) gluttony, drunkenness, and fornication. Lacking the concepts of orthodoxy and dogma, being sceptical of claims to inspiration, and restricting priestly authority to narrowly defined areas, the Greek community adjusted its religious attitudes to its social needs. It is more profitable to try to understand Greek religion in the light of what happened at festivals than to try to force upon the artistic aspect of festivals an interpretation founded on religious preconceptions.

The religious element in drama is the same as the religious element in epic and in pre-dramatic lyric poetry: myth is not about ordinary people, but about the relationships between deities and the 'heroes' and 'heroines' who were often 'half-gods', children of a union between a deity and a mortal or the descendants of such a union. These heroes and heroines were, in local cults and on a restricted scale, recipients, like deities, of prayer and sacrifice. Myth therefore has a commemorative aspect, reminding us by example of divine power and super-human achievement. Although some deities are in some respects personifications of forces and powers constantly active in human life, it will not do to treat deities in tragedy as 'only' personifications or symbols. Euripides' *Hippolytus* is a case in point. Phaedra, the wife of Theseus, falls in love with Hippolytus, Theseus' son by a previous marriage. The prologue to the play is spoken by the goddess Aphrodite, whose province is sexual desire. So far, so good; a woman may unpredictably fall in love with her stepson, and if this happens it is likely to generate a train of tragic events. But Aphrodite explains that she has caused Phaedra to fall in love because Hippolytus is obdurately chaste, a devotee of the virgin huntress-goddess Artemis and hostile to Aphrodite. Well, if a very handsome young man hates the idea of sex, some tragic events may be in store for him too, but it would be hard to extract from the play with any confidence the generalization that if a young man has a girl-friend his stepmother will not fall in love with him. Aphrodite makes it quite clear that she will use poor Phaedra simply as a means of taking her own revenge on Hippolytus, and this tells us at the start that the play is not 'about' the consequences either of unpredictable passion or of obdurate chastity; it could more plausibly be said to be about what the divine person Aphrodite does to the human person Hippolytus. Phaedra commits suicide, leaving a letter accusing Hippolytus of raping her. Theseus curses Hippolytus, calling upon his own father, the god Poseidon (who had once promised him the fulfilment of three curses). Hippolytus departs into exile, and Poseidon fulfils the curse by making a dreadful bull appear from the sea, so that Hippolytus' horses panic and he is fatally injured. At the end of the play the goddess Artemis appears and tells Theseus the truth; father and son are reconciled before

Hippolytus dies. There is no way of 'translating' this story into non-religious terms, no way of reducing Poseidon, the bull, and Artemis to symbols. Again, it might seem open to us to interpret Euripides' *Bacchae* in terms of conflict between rational order (represented by Pentheus) and the irrational violence (Dionysus) which demands periodic expression. But if we take it so, how do we fit in the miraculous earthquake which releases Dionysus from imprisonment? And at the end of the play Dionysus, appearing in glory, links the story of the play with other ingredients of the complex of myths about the family to which Pentheus belonged:

You, Cadmus, will be turned into a serpent; and your wife Harmonia, daughter of Ares, whom you, a mortal, married, will be transformed from human shape into a snake's. And with your wife you will drive a chariot drawn by bullocks — such is the oracle of Zeus — leading a barbarian host. And many a city will you sack with your numberless army; but when they have ravaged the oracular seat of Apollo, disaster will fall upon their homeward journey. But you and Harmonia Ares will save and put you to live in the Land of the Blessed.

(Euripides, *Bacchae* 1330–9)

Cadmus, Pentheus' grandfather, had not opposed (far from it) the introduction of the orgiastic worship of Dionysus into Thebes, but the god's anger has fallen on the whole community. Such were the mythical data which Euripides inherited, and it is arguable that the extent to which a poet manipulated the data available to him depended less on his religious principles or on any simple, overriding moral 'lesson' which he wished to teach than on the theatrical possibilities which formed in his mind when he contemplated the ramifications and implications of the inherited material.

Dionysus at the end of *Bacchae* is a *deus ex machina*, a term which has its origin in the Greek *mēkhanē*, the crane used to represent a deity as flying down from the sky. The introduction of a deity in this way is sometimes used to resolve an impasse reached in the action of the play at human level. In Sophocles' *Philoctetes* Neoptolemus, charged with tricking Philoctetes into coming to the Greek camp at Troy, takes pity on him, abjures the deceit which political duty requires of him, and agrees instead to take Philoctetes home. What then is to become of the prophecy that the Greeks will never capture Troy without the bow of Philoctetes? It will be fulfilled; for Herakles (a hero who became a god on the death of his mortal body) manifests himself to Neoptolemus and Philoctetes, bringing them the command of Zeus. The resolution of the action in Euripides' *Orestes* is even more abrupt. Orestes, condemned by the citizens of Argos for his matricide, has his sword at the throat of Menelaus' daughter Hermione, determined to kill her unless Menelaus will save him from punishment. Electra and Pylades, Orestes' inseparable companion, are ready to set fire to the palace; Menelaus raises the cry for help; then the turmoil is suddenly 'frozen' by Apollo, who confirms Orestes in his patrimony and commands him to marry the girl he has been on the point of murdering.

The introduction of a deity to resolve the action is particularly Euripidean (Herakles in *Philoctetes* is the only example in the surviving work of Sophocles), and an opening prologue by a deity, explaining the situation to the audience, is peculiar to Euripides (*Bacchae, Hippolytus, Ion*). Aeschylus, following the precedent set by the debates, quarrels, and intrigues of the gods in many passages of Homer, confidently handles divine characters in conflict and humanizes them. In *Eumenides* Orestes, pursued by the Furies, comes to Athens, and the Furies agree that Athena shall arbitrate. Athena convenes a jury of citizens, over which she presides; the case is argued on the one side by the Furies, on the other by Apollo, and neither side is free of the arrogance and venom which characterize human litigants. When it is time for the jury to vote, Athena (who was born, motherless, from the head of Zeus, and is a virgin warrior-goddess) announces that she will vote for Orestes' acquittal:

Now it remains for me to give my judgement. I will put this vote on Orestes' side. For I was not born of a mother; I commend the male in all things (save that I will not marry) with all my heart; I am wholly the father's. So I will not give greater weight to the death of a wife who killed her husband, guardian of the house. Orestes wins, even if the votes of the jury are equal.

(Aeschylus, *Eumenides* 734–41)

II

Every picture, statue, play or film we see, every novel we read, necessarily contributes to the formation of our moral character, just as much as — often more potently than — our practical relations with people and things. Since the myths which are the subject-matter of Greek tragedy are stories of war, murder, suicide, adultery, and extreme manifestations of arrogance and ambition, it is natural for us to ask what the playwright is telling us about those things through the medium of a particular myth. It is not uncommon to ask whether Greek tragedy as a whole was intended by the playwrights, and accepted by its original audience, as a vehicle for moral lessons and warnings. Simplistic answers are sometimes offered to these questions, especially in terms of divine law and the peril of incurring divine punishment by ignoring the Delphic maxims 'Know yourself' (that is, 'Recognize your situation and your limitations') and 'Nothing in excess' (that is, 'Set a limit to the realization of your wishes and ambitions'). The reality is more subtle. The individual personalities and predilections of deities, the nexus of friendships and enmities attributed in myth to each deity, the freedom of a Greek to entertain and express his own opinion on the justice or injustice of any given divine action, the patent absence of any moral lesson from the sequences of events constituting many Greek myths, all discourage the ambition to formulate any sweeping generalization about the religious, moral, and social function of Greek tragedy. Yet an audience's moral and aesthetic responses to the development of a serious story on stage are intimately interconnected, as Aristotle fully recognized in discussing (*Poetics* 13–15) the dramatic effectiveness of different relationships between character and fortune, and a tragedy which does not make us think about good and evil could fairly be regarded as an empty spectacle. The average member of Sophocles' audience might not have said that in so many words; 'What is tragedy?' and 'What is the essence of the tragic?' sound portentous questions in English, but 'What is *tragōidiā*?' would not have sounded portentous to a Greek. He would have told us firstly, that it is drama, as opposed to other kinds of poetry; secondly, that it is an ingredient of certain festivals of Dionysus (for a Greek would tend to define a literary genre in terms of the occasions to which it belonged); and thirdly, that it is serious, as opposed to satyr-plays and comedy. He would not mean by 'serious' that it always leaves us oppressed by grief and compassion. Some tragedies do (for example, Sophocles' *Antigone* and *Oedipus the King*), but others (for example, Aeschylus' *Eumenides*) achieve a profoundly satisfying resolution of the issues which they have presented, while others again (for example, Euripides' *Helen* and *Iphigenia among the Tauri*) take us through adventures full of peril and despair to a 'happy ending'. But all alike concern issues of life and death. Aristotle's *Poetics* has much to say — not all of it clear (to us) but none of it pretentious — on how tragedy achieves its effect. But he writes as a critic, with primarily philosophical and scientific interests, looking back on the history of an art-form two or three generations after its zenith, and before reading him it is prudent that we should form some ideas of our own, on the basis of our own acquaintance with the plays, about the relation between aesthetic, moral, and intellectual aspects of fifth-century tragedy.

The choral songs make a good starting-point. Greek myths lend themselves very unequally to treatment in the form of Greek tragedy. In Euripides' *Bacchae* the flight of the women from their homes under the inspiration of Dionysus is an essential ingredient of the story, so that a chorus of women following in the train of the god is virtually dictated. In Aeschylus' *Suppliants* the issue of the play is the fate of the chorus itself (the daughters of Danaus). However, there are other stories, such as the return of Orestes to avenge his father, to which a chorus is anything but indispensable, and some (obvious examples are Phaedra's secret passion for her stepson in Euripides' *Hippolytus* and Medea's decision to murder her children in Euripides' *Medea*) in which the presence of a chorus observably creates awkward problems for the dramatist. In so far as the content of a choral passage is sometimes elicited by the preceding action, there is a temptation to treat the chorus as commenting, reflecting, even preaching, on the 'text' furnished by the action — a temptation to believe that through his choruses the poet (to put it crudely) is telling us what to think. That, however, is an aspect of tragedy on which the Greeks themselves make no remark. In Aristophanes' *Frogs,* where the ghost of

Aeschylus and the ghost of Euripides contend for the throne of poetry in the underworld, the moral effect of tragedy on its audience and the validity of judging a poet by that effect are taken for granted; the effect is sought, however, not in the reflections voiced in choral songs, but in the behaviour of individual characters and the sentiments uttered by them. Plato's criticism of tragedy in the *Republic* is also focused on its presentation of deities and heroes as unworthy, even dangerous paradigms; we would not infer from what he says that tragedy had a chorus. Aristotle equally says nothing of choral reflections when discussing the moral responses of the audience. Part of the reason why a feature of Greek tragedy which seems to us so distinctive and important played no part in the Greeks' own discussion of the moral aspect of tragedy is that telling myths and drawing solemn warnings or salutary generalizations from them had always been a feature of choral lyric; it was thus not a characteristic element of tragedy at all, but an element shared by drama with other kinds of poetry, and therefore unlikely to be mentioned in comparing playwrights or in discussing the specific effects and functions of tragedy. Other reasons will emerge from an examination of some specimen choral passages.

In Aeschylus' *Suppliants* the daughters of Danaus, fleeing from Egypt in abhorrence of their cousins, who claim them in marriage, come to Argos (their ancestral land) in the hope of sanctuary. But they cannot know what 'the desire of Zeus' will be.

> It is no easy quarry.
> All ways it flames, even in darkness;
> black is the fate it brings to mortal men.
> When by the nod of Zeus' head a fulfilment is decreed,
> it falls on sure feet, not toppling back.
> For through bush and tangle
> thread the tracks of his thought,
> hard for the eye to mark.
> Down from the high tower of hope
> he throws men in welter of death,
> girding on no might of weapons.
> Divinity is not laborious.
> From his seat on his holy throne

unmoving, none the less — who knows how? —
he executes his will.

(Aeschylus, *Suppliants* 87–103)

What they say, reduced to the simplest words, is: we do not know
what Zeus will do, but whatever he decides should happen, he
will cause it to happen. This is not a novel utterance, and no
sinner will be turned to repentance by the declaration of desper-
ate suppliants that their ancestral god is all-powerful. But this
very simple content is clothed in a succession of vivid, disturbing
images; in the present case, a literary and textual problem has
been generated by a modern proposal that 'all ways . . . to mortal
men' and 'for through bush . . . to mark' should be transposed,
and the problem is one on which the Greekless reader, too, may
profitably reflect. That the chorus's religious generalization
concentrates on the destructiveness of Zeus ('black is the fate . . .'
and 'down from the high tower . . .') is attributable not to
bitterness on the part of Aeschylus but to their own situation:
they are the weak in flight from the strong.

In Sophocles' *Oedipus the King* Thebes is stricken with plague,
and the Delphic oracle has declared that the Thebans must
discover and kill or expel the murderer of their former king,
Laius. The blind seer Tiresias, summoned by Oedipus, asserts
that Oedipus is himself the murderer. Oedipus in fury suspects
that his brother-in-law Creon has bribed Tiresias to utter these
allegations as part of a plot to overthrow him. The chorus is
dismayed. Oedipus saved Thebes by solving the riddle of the
Sphinx, in consequence of which he became king and married
Laius' widow; they owe him only gratitude and loyalty; yet the
prestige of Tiresias as a seer is formidable. What are they to
think?

> And yet though Zeus and Apollo
> understand all and know the fate of mortals,
> whether a seer is worth more than I
> there is no sure judging.
> The skill of one man may surpass another's.
> But never will I, before I see the utterance proved,
> assent to accusation of Oedipus.
> For I remember when the Winged Maiden was his adversary,
> and his skill was seen;

in the proof, he won my city's heart.
Never, then, in my judgement will he stand condemned.
(Sophocles, *Oedipus the King* 497–511)

Their obstinate faith proves to be unjustified, for Oedipus is indeed the murderer of Laius, and this chorus is no mouthpiece of the poet but a group of Thebans voicing the feelings which they would obviously voice at the point which the unfolding of the story has reached.

Another famous Sophoclean choral song illustrates other ways in which the tragic poets could use their choruses. In Sophocles' *Antigone* Creon, ruler of Thebes, has condemned Antigone to death because she disobeyed his command and gave burial to her brother. Creon's son Haemon, betrothed to Antigone, recommends that she should be pardoned, but this is angrily rejected by Creon, and father and son part in irreconcilable bitterness. The chorus reflects not on the obstinacy of Creon in maintaining his authority, but on the passion, Haemon's love for Antigone, which (the chorus implies) underlies and has generated the quarrel.

> Love unconquerable in battle,
> Love, ravager of wealth,
> lurking watchful in the soft cheeks of a girl,
> beyond the seas you go your ways
> and in the dwellings of the countryside.
> No immortal can outpace you,
> nor any human creature of a day;
> who has you, has his wits no more.
> You twist the heart of the righteous
> aside into unrighteousness, and ill follows.
> You have stirred this strife
> which now sunders the tie of blood.
> Desire kindled in the eyes
> for the body of a bride
> is hoisted victorious,
> enthroned beside the great ordinances
> in the roots of the world.
> One smile of the goddess Aphrodite,
> and there is no fight left.
> (Sophocles, *Antigone* 781–801)

If the preceding scene had been lost and we had to reconstruct it from this song, we would probably go badly astray. Haemon did not come to ask openly for a favour on behalf of his intended bride, but to warn his father of the murmurings of the citizens and to remind him of the limits which wise authority observes. He addressed his father with the greatest respect and circumspection, and it was Creon who provoked the quarrel by committing the gravest of parental sins, refusal to listen seriously to what one's children say seriously. To that extent 'you twist . . . the tie of blood', which sounds like a condemnation of Haemon for filial impiety, is discordant with what has been played out on stage. The chorus makes the tacit assumption that if Haemon had not been in love with Antigone he would not have troubled to warn Creon of public opinion (even, perhaps, that his assessment of public opinion would have been different), and we may well be invited to share that assumption. But the choral song has other purposes to serve. In the first place, it is a foreboding of what is to come, for Creon will lose his son; Antigone, immured alive in a tomb, hangs herself, and Haemon commits suicide, beside her corpse, unreconciled with his father. Secondly, it is a hymn to Love (that is to say, to Eros, the personification of sexual love) which includes ingredients irrelevant to the action of the play ('ravager of wealth', 'beyond the seas . . . countryside' and 'no immortal . . .') but thoroughly familiar in poems and speeches (and no doubt in ordinary talk) about Love. Except for the reference in 'this strife which now sunders . . .', the hymn could stand as an independent poem.

This kind of exploitation of the poetic opportunities afforded by a choral passage became increasingly common in tragedy. The song may be, as it were, hooked on to the play by making the chorus express a wish to escape from a distressing predicament; 'would that I were not here, but in *X*' launches a song about *X*. In Euripides' *Helen* (1301–68) a long hymn to the goddess Cybele intervenes between two stages in the development of the plot formed by Helen and Menelaus to escape from Egypt, and if it is relevant to that plot, or to anything else in the play, no one has yet succeeded in explaining what its relevance is. In fourth-century tragedy, as in fourth-century comedy, the complete independence of choral song from dramatic action was widely accepted.

All these considerations show that it is wrong to treat choral utterance as a direct indication of what the dramatist wishes us to think about the enacted story. It makes no better sense to extract from the utterances of individual characters their creator's 'philosophy of life'. The ancients themselves have set us a bad example in taking lines out of context. In Euripides' *Hippolytus* Phaedra's old nurse divulges her mistress's passion to Hippolytus himself, having first of all persuaded him to swear on oath that he will never reveal what she is about to tell him. When he has heard what she has to tell, he is outraged, and cries his outrage at the top of his voice. The nurse, terrified, reminds him of his oath, and he replies: 'My tongue has sworn, but my heart is unsworn.' (Euripides, *Hippolytus* 612).

The line became notorious, and is used in a joke against Euripides in Aristophanes, *Frogs* 1471. According to an anecdote in Aristotle, *Rhetoric* iii 15.8, a man engaged in litigation against Euripides suggested to the jury that no one could trust the oath of a poet who had penned a line which appeared to justify the breaking of an oath when one's 'heart' did not wish to keep it. In fact, however, Hippolytus, once his rage has cooled, does keep his oath, going into exile under his father's curse and under the shadow of a monstrously false accusation, rather than commit perjury. The notorious line is therefore the kind of thing that someone like Hippolytus might well say in that kind of situation, rather as Creon in Sophocles, *Antigone* 769, beside himself with rage after his quarrel with Haemon, condemns to death both Antigone and her sister Ismene and then shamefacedly revokes the sentence on the innocent Ismene when the chorus-leader has made a shocked protest.

The extent of the tragic poets' interest in characterization has become a controversial issue in our own time; there are passages and scenes which can be interpreted one way on the assumption that their psychological realism is profound, but differently on the assumption that the poet was more interested in the polarization of conflict and the exploitation of the issues raised by a particular scene irrespective of its relationship to the rest of the play. It is undesirable that the question should be treated as if one answer to it were universally applicable to all Greek tragedy. It is also unfortunate that a popular modern confusion between psycho-

logy and psychoanalysis has encouraged the idea that to seek
psychological realism in Greek tragedy is anachronistic; all that is
being sought is evidence that the poets were good at perceiving
and portraying the ways in which people actually think and feel.
The reader, if he is prepared to keep an open mind, can decide for
himself which characters seem to him intelligible as people,
which utterances seem to him realistic, and in what circumstances the motivation ascribed to a character shows the dramatist to be perceptive. An element of stock characterization is not
wholly absent from the tragic treatment of myth; Menelaus and
Odysseus tend to be portrayed unsympathetically (though the
magnanimity of Odysseus in Sophocles, *Ajax* 1316ff. and the
unselfish compassion of Menelaus in Euripides, *Iphigenia at Aulis*
471ff. forbid a stronger word than 'tend'), and the Athenian hero
Theseus is invested with the qualities which the Athenians
admired.

We see Theseus in Euripides' *Herakles Mad* at a moment when
Herakles, who once saved him from the underworld, has recovered from the fearful fit of insanity which led him to murder his
wife and children.

THESEUS Why do you wag your hand at me and sign 'murder'? So that
the pollution of your voice may not fall upon me? I am not worried at
sharing your misfortune, for once I shared your glory. Think of that time
when you brought me from the land of the dead and up into the light. I
detest a debt of friendship that fades with age, and anyone who is ready
to take his share of another's blessings but not to sail with his friends
when they are in trouble. Rise up, uncover your face, my poor friend,
look at me. A noble man endures it when the gods throw him down; he
does not refuse to face his fall.

HERAKLES Theseus, you see this battle I fought against my own
children?

THESEUS I heard about it; and now I see the horrors at which you point.

HERAKLES Why then did you uncover my face to the sun?

THESEUS Why! You, a mortal, cannot inflict defilement on what is
divine.

HERAKLES O Theseus, be warned, my defilement is unholy – flee from
it!

THESEUS No evil spirit infects friend from friend.

(Euripides, *Herakles Mad* 1218–34)

Euripides is not saying that the doctrine of pollution by contact with murderers is false, nor even that friendship is an inoculation against it; he is depicting a man who.puts courage, loyalty, gratitude, and sensibility above the danger of pollution and uses every argument he can think of (as one would, in such circumstances) to bring Herakles back into real life.

Argument is an intellectual process, and Greek tragedy sometimes incurs the danger of 'intellectualizing' issues to which in reality incoherent emotion would be a more probable response. A combination of independent factors creates this danger. One is the formality of structure of Greek tragedy, largely concealed by translation: many of its choral songs are constructed in symmetrical pairs of stanzas, and in dialogue the complete verse is usually treated as the minimum unit of utterance, so that an interchange may consist of a succession of alternate lines for over two minutes. A second factor is the exceptionally strong interest of the Greeks in oratory as an art-form, and not least in the challenge and response of prosecutor and defendant in a court of law. Moreover, the fifth century B.C., and particularly its second half, was a time at which great intellectual excitement was generated by the realization that many traditional attitudes and assumptions were unable to stand up to the attack of reason. The articulation of bold and new ideas was attractive for its own sake, and the dramatist was tempted to transfer personal conflict to the plane of debate.

Euripides yielded to the temptation more obviously than Sophocles and Aeschylus, but the difference is one of degree. Both in Sophocles' *Electra* and in Euripides' *Electra* we see a confrontation between daughter and hated mother, and in both the confrontation is organized as a set-piece debate. In Sophocles Clytaemnestra, beginning in a threatening tone, slides (520–7) into a plea of justification (528–48) for her murder of Agamemnon and ends (549–51) with what is in effect a challenge to Electra to refute her. 'If you allow me,' says Electra (552–5) 'I would like to give the truth.' Clytaemnestra replies (556ff.): 'Yes, I do allow you . . .'; whereupon Electra (beginning 'This is what I say to you' [558]) attacks Clytaemnestra's plea point by point (558–609). In Euripides, Clytaemnestra, tricked into coming to the poor home where Electra lives with her peasant husband, makes a speech of over thirty lines justifying her murder of Agamemnon, and ends it with (1048ff.): 'Speak, if you wish to. Be frank, and argue against me that your father did not justly die.' Electra, having obtained a repetition of the assurance that she is free to speak her mind, does so (1060ff.): 'I'll speak then. And this is the opening of my preface . . .'. These are examples of personal hatred transmuted into debate. Importation of debate into a context in which the precondition of personal conflict does not exist is best illustrated by a scene in Euripides' *Suppliants*. This play, unlike Aeschylus' *Suppliants* (which concerns the flight of the daughters of Danaus to Argos), shows the arrival at Athens of the mothers of the heroes who died in Polynices' vain attempt to capture Thebes. They are accompanied by Adrastus, king of Argos, who had commanded the expedition, and they beg Theseus, as leading man of Athens, to demand from Thebes the surrender of the bodies of the dead heroes for proper burial. Theseus, having at first rejected the appeal on the grounds that Adrastus' expedition was unjustified and its fate no business of Athens', yields to the entreaty of his compassionate mother, obtains the agreement of the Athenian assembly, and prepares to send his demand to Thebes. At this point there arrives a Theban herald, whose first words (399) are 'Who is the king of this land?' Theseus replies

In the first place, you began your speech on a wrong note, seeking a 'king' here, for this city is not ruled by one man; it is free. The people rules, with annual change of office, not giving the biggest share to wealth, but the poor man too has equal rights. (403–8)

The herald then attacks democracy, beginning (409–11): 'A false move; you've lost a piece to me. For the city from which I have come is governed by one man, not by a mob . . .'. Theseus retorts (426–8): 'A clever herald, this, with such a lot to say! Now that you've made your speech on the motion, listen to mine; for it was you who set up a debate . . .', and voices the arguments, familiar to us elsewhere in Greek literature, against monarchy and in favour of democracy. Only after thirty lines does he ask the herald what his message from Thebes is. In this instance explicit allusion is made to the transformation of a potentially simple demand and response into a debate on rival political structures.

In some instances we hear one side of a case only, when all that a character has ever (we may imagine) thought about a given topic is coherently articulated at a moment of strong emotion. Medea's speech in Euripides, *Medea* 230–51, ending with 'I had rather stand three times in line of battle than give birth once', is the most powerful surviving indictment of the discrimination against women which characterized Greek society and, in general, Greek thought. We do not know what its original audience thought of it (Euripides' portrayal of women gained him the reputation of a woman-hater), nor do we know whether Euripides believed that the roles of the sexes in society should be radically altered. We only know that he put into the mouth of Medea arguments available and welcome to an unjustly treated woman, arguments to which he himself and others might have replied (rather as the chorus-leader says to Clytaemnestra in Euripides' *Electra* 1051) 'What you have said is just, *but . . .*'

Before we can think profitably about what a given Greek tragedy 'means', what it is 'about', we have to see it or read it from beginning to end, and we have to relate it to the dramatist's work as a whole and to the ideas and sentiments known to be prevalent in the Greek world at the time of its production. A modern audience readily discerns 'anti-war' sentiment in Euripides' *Trojan Women*; this audience is less familiar with the bellicose chauvinism of the same poet's *Suppliants* and *Heraclidae* or with the exalted willingness of Iphigenia in *Iphigenia at Aulis* to accept the role of sacrificial victim for patriotic motives. It is also unlikely to have heard of the speech of a queen in the lost play *Erechtheus* (the speech is cited by a fourth-century orator) declaring that her daughter is owed to the state, not to her, and must be sacrificed if an oracle makes that the condition of victory. There is no reason to suppose that Euripides changed his mind or that he was less 'sincere' on some occasions than on others. Being a Greek, he did not think that war is *either* glorious *or* cruel, but recognized that it is both, and that the experience of one of its aspects is neither more nor less 'real' than the experience of any other of its aspects.

III

The tragic poets made effective use of two religious concepts, the curse and the familial inheritance of a curse, of which the former is a constant in Greek culture (for a curse is simply a special kind of prayer), while the latter belongs to a particular stage of Greek thinking about the relation between religion and morality. The early belief that the gods cause an unrighteous man to suffer disaster was naturally unstable, since much everyday observation refutes it. It was modified into a belief (made explicit in a poem of Solon early in the sixth century B.C.) that divine punishment might fall not on the unrighteous man himself but on his children or descendants. This doctrine, too, is objectionable, since it entails the infliction of suffering on blameless individuals, and in the classical period it gradually yielded to a widespread belief that the individual's soul is rewarded or punished in the afterlife according to his conduct on earth (a belief not wholly unknown, but by no means prominent, in the archaic period). Many Greek myths, portraying as they do outrage and bloodshed in successive generations of the same family, are well suited to interpretation in terms of inherited punishment, and tragedy contains virtually no reference to judgement of the soul after death. Thyestes seduces the wife of his brother Atreus. Atreus kills Thyestes' children, cooks them, and serves them up to their father. Thyestes curses the family of Atreus. Atreus' son, Agamemnon, leads the Greeks against Troy. At Aulis the fleet is penned in by adverse winds, and Calchas the seer asserts that Artemis is angry with the Greeks and can be appeased only if Agamemnon sacrifices to her his daughter Iphigenia. He does so, and the fleet sails. At home in Argos Agamemnon's wife Clytaemnestra takes Aegisthus, son of Thyestes, as a lover, and when at last Agamemnon returns victorious from Troy they murder him. In Aeschylus' *Agamemnon* a note of foreboding is struck at the very beginning, even as the watchman on the roof sees the distant beacon which proclaims the fall of Troy. In the choral passage which follows, the circumstances which led to the pitiable death of Iphigenia are described, and the chorus's revulsion against it leads them (250–7) to speculation on what the future will bring and to heartfelt but consciously helpless expression of the hope that all will be well. When Agamemnon comes home, he brings with him Cassandra, a Trojan princess, as captive concubine. She is clairvoyant; she sees a vision of murdered and mutilated children, and the chorus admits, first allusively (1098ff.) and then plainly (1242ff.) that they know what she means. She also foresees Agamemnon's murder, in visions which become increasingly specific. Only at the end of the play does Aegisthus appear and declare that Thyestes cursed the family of Atreus. At this point we can construct a causal sequence which interrelates human and divine action: the gods heard Thyestes' curse; they brought about the predicament which caused Agamemnon to sacrifice his daughter; this made his wife his enemy and sealed his fate; and we know from Cassandra's prophecies (1279–85) that the son of Agamemnon and Clytaemnestra will return one day to avenge his father.

But what kind of causal sequence is this? Men can never know for sure whether the gods have accepted a curse or not; nor can we know whether a disaster which we undergo is the manifestation of a curse. Does Aeschylus mean us to believe that Agamemnon's decision to sacrifice his daughter was a free choice, or that it was inescapable? Different interpreters of the play have given different answers to that question; perhaps Aeschylus meant us to do just that. Was the predicament that led to the sacrifice generated by the curse or by deities angry at the impending fate of Troy? Was it inevitable that Clytaemnestra should never forgive the sacrifice, or did Aegisthus seduce her? (Pindar poses, and does not answer, that question [*Pythian Odes* 11.22ff.]). In her confrontation with the chorus after the murder, she boasts, threatens, pleads justification, and at one point (one only) speaks as if she were no more than the instrument of the divine fulfilment of Thyestes' curse (*Agamemnon* 1475–504), a claim to which the chorus first responds with indignant rebuttal, then at once wavers in uncertainty.

There are other myths, notably the 'Theban cycle' concerning Oedipus, his father Laius, and his sons Eteocles and Polynices, in which the concept of the curse and its inheritance can be imported or omitted. Oedipus certainly cursed his sons, and the fulfilment of the curse is the theme of Aeschylus' *Seven against Thebes* (cf. Sophocles, *Oedipus at Colonus* 1370–82). Oedipus' own parricide and incest could have been treated as the manifestation of an inherited curse, but see how Sophocles makes him speak in a furious response to Creon:

My murder, my marriage, disasters — the words trip off your tongue. Who bore that burden of misery? I did, but through no choice of mine; it was the gods' will that it should happen. Had they — who knows? — some cause of wrath against my family long ago?

(Sophocles, *Oedipus at Colonus* 962–5)

Oedipus does not know, and cannot know, whether or not he has inherited a curse. The best-known version of a myth may state the matter boldly, and if we know that, we look ahead to the completion of a sequence of events which for characters and chorus, at any given moment in a play, is incomplete. It is *their* experience of uncertainty, anxiety or blind confidence which tragedy, by enacting the words and deeds of a myth in temporal sequence, invites us to share.

Oedipus, in the passage cited, denies responsibility and refuses to be treated, in accordance with the normal Greek revulsion against parricide and incest, as a defiled object (Sophocles' Theseus in *Oedipus at Colonus,* as sensitive and compassionate as Euripides' Theseus in *Herakles Mad* some years earlier, discards that revulsion). There is no suggestion that the gods' justice is morally better or wiser than man's. The notion that the gods punish wickedness is a great consolation when we are ourselves innocent and indignant sufferers, and one of the themes of Aeschylus' *Persians,* that the Persian invaders of Greece incurred disaster because they destroyed the gods' sanctuaries (807ff.), will certainly have received the audience's moral assent. It is however blended (828ff.) with a different notion, familiar to us later from Herodotus (for example vii 10.ε.1.), that power, wealth, and ambition suffice to incur divine resentment. The fact that the chief personages of Greek tragedy are heroes and heroines (or, in *Persians,* the most powerful monarch in the world) greatly enhances the dramatic effect of their humiliating fall, which pre-dramatic poetry also on occasion treated as a paradigm of human weakness in the face of arbitrary fate or inscrutable divinity. In the case of Oedipus, the effect of his fall is enhanced also by the rapidity of his rise: a lonely wanderer from

Corinth, he became king of Thebes, and the revelation of his parentage makes him a lonely wanderer again, blinded in self-hatred and foreseeing only shame and ruin for his children.

Positive hostility to the divine government of the world appears to be a central theme of *Prometheus Bound*, a strange and powerful play, the traditional attribution of which to Aeschylus becomes more difficult the more fully its technical aspects (language, metre, stagecraft) are investigated. Prometheus, once ally of Zeus, is fettered to a lonely rock by Zeus because he opposed the desire of Zeus to obliterate mankind. It is inevitable that in Prometheus' own words Zeus should be treated as a cruel and ungrateful tyrant but the portrayal of Hermes, messenger of Zeus, as a bullying lackey is the playwright's deliberate choice. In Euripides' *Ion* the starting-point of the story is the brutal rape of the human girl Creusa by the god Apollo, but (by contrast with *Prometheus Bound*) the just resentment of the victim is dispelled by the unforeseen outcome of the train of events which that rape set in motion. There are no easy answers to the conflicts which form the issues of Greek tragedies: conflicts of loyalty between family, friends, and nation, or between simple human impulse and recognition that the gods will have their way. The tragic poets understood how to use the manifold potentialities of inherited myth in a manner which makes us feel and think about issues transcending the particular data of myth.

5 Comedy

The names of comic dramatists whose plays were performed at
the City Dionysia at Athens were not embodied in a permanent
record until 486 B.C. It is quite possible (cf. p. 50) that humorous
dramatic performances had played some part in the festival for a
very long time — possible, that is, that comedy is far older than
tragedy but long regarded as ephemeral, topical, and not to be
perpetuated in written texts. Aristophanes is the only comic poet
of the fifth century B.C. whose plays we can read now; eleven (out
of at least forty which he wrote) have survived. He first produced
a play in 427, and of the surviving eleven the earliest, *Acharnians*,
is datable to 425. We know something, through citations and
fragments, about some comedies produced in the period 440–425,
but as we move back in time the evidence dwindles rapidly, and
very little indeed can be said with assurance about the nature of
the comedy contemporary with Aeschylean tragedy. Our ignorance is a pity, because the earlier Aristophanic plays give us the
impression that comedy as he inherited it was a compound of at
least two elements originally distinct.

One of these elements is a chorus (of twenty-four) which may
represent human beings (for example, *Acharnians, Babylonians*) but
also, and often, other creatures (for example, *Birds*) and personified entities (for example, *Clouds*). This was certainly an old
art-form, because we find on sixth-century Attic vases pictures of
men dressed up as horses or birds and dancing to the accompaniment of a piper. The tradition remained strong throughout
Aristophanes' lifetime, as we see from the titles of his *Wasps* and
Frogs. These two plays are not 'about' wasps or frogs, but in the
former the chorus represents old Athenian jurors dressed as
wasps to symbolize their disposition, and in the latter the
frog-chorus appears only in one scene near the beginning of the
play, being thereafter replaced by a different chorus, the souls of

the initiated in the underworld. About the middle of a comedy the actors are all off-stage and the chorus addresses itself directly to the audience, interspersing the passages of address with song and dance. In this portion of the play (the 'parabasis') the characters and dramatic action are ignored, and if we see in the rest of the play a sustained and vigorous topical 'message' we find to our surprise that precisely in the parabasis, where we might have expected the message to be spelled out in direct form, it is suspended. The chorus does not cease to be (for example) birds or clouds; but for the duration of the parabasis they are no longer birds or clouds participating in the fictitious sequence of events which constitutes the action of the play, but birds or clouds visiting Athens on the occasion of the festival. So, for example:

When we were all set to leave for Athens, the Moon met us and told us to give you and your allies her greetings, but then she said that she's annoyed with you . . . You don't stick to the calendar properly, but muck about with it this way and that, so that the gods keep on telling her off, when they're cheated of a dinner and go back home, missing the festival that they were expecting through counting up the days . . .

(Aristophanes, *Clouds* 607–10, 615–19)

This is a felicitous way of talking about the manipulations of the calendar which had occurred at the time when *Clouds* was produced, and unlike the pious indignation which earlier this century resisted the seasonal alteration of clocks as 'interfering with God's time'. The Aristophanic parabasis never loses a certain lightness of touch, and it is often devoted in part to self-advertisement, coupled with denigration of the other poets competing for the first prize. In *Acharnians* Aristophanes uses the fact that he lived on Aegina to create an agreeably fantastic picture of international relations.

When the king of Persia was sounding out the embassy which came to him from Sparta, he asked them first which side had the upper hand at sea, and secondly, which side had been vilified by our poet — for, he said, *they* had become much the better men and would win all their battles, if they had the poet as their adviser. That's why the Spartans want you to make peace, that's why they want Aegina back; they're not worrying about that island, it's so that they can rob you of the poet.

(Aristophanes, *Acharnians* 647–53)

The second major ingredient of Aristophanic comedy is the enacted story, and here, with no Attic vase-paintings to offer direct help, reconstruction of literary affinities is more problematic. There is some evidence to suggest that comic drama existed in parts of the Doric-speaking world at least as early as in Attica, and conceivably earlier. At the beginning of the fifth century Epicharmus, a citizen of Syracuse, composed comic dialogues in dramatic form. How regularly they included a part for a chorus, or whether they were actually performed in a theatre, we do not know for sure; but the surviving fragments and citations reveal many characteristics later to be found in Aristophanic comedy, including jocular treatment of religious and mythological motifs and dialogues not only charged with natural vigour but also tinged with vulgarity. The tradition established by Epicharmus continued independently in the West, partly as 'mimes' (comic scenes intended for the reader rather than the stage) and partly as a local comic drama on which, it seems, the increasing elegance and subtlety of Attic comedy in the later classical period had little influence. Epicharmus himself had a reputation as a wise man, and some poetry of a moralizing and philosophical character, composed in his dialect and style, was wrongly attributed to him in later times.

The plot of an Aristophanic comedy is rooted in the occasion of performance; unlike tragedy, which re-enacts an event conceived as belonging to the remote past, a comedy enacts something which could happen, if imagination is allowed to triumph over the obstacles interposed by reality, any moment now. Burlesque versions of myths were not uncommon in the comic theatre, but we know of them only through citations and summaries; the plays we have in full, from the fifth century, are all, with varying degrees of precision, topical. Even when the theme of the play is not itself an issue of the moment, allusions to people and events familiar to the audience spring up in the dialogue of the characters and the songs of the chorus, sometimes virtually as asides, sometimes to make the climax of a joke. We are not allowed to forget for long that we are watching people dressed up for our entertainment, for comic dialogue is charged with references to the theatre itself ('Over there, in the wings!' or 'Watch it, Props, the crane's wobbling!'), to the audience ('There's Sosias telling Dercylus he thinks the old man's an alcoholic') and to the play as a play ('Well, now, I'd better tell the audience what this is all about'). Moreover, the dialogue on occasion takes a turn which suggests that the author is making his actors step outside their roles within the plot and play out a joke in a manner which we associate more with revue than with drama.

II

It is quite possible for a work of art to be simultaneously dramatic and topical without thereby advocating or deprecating any particular action by the community on any particular issue. If, however, it also employs ridicule, satire, and personal invective, not impartially in the depiction of a conflict between fully characterized adversaries, but one-sidedly in pronouncements addressed to the audience or in the verbal armoury of a 'hero' achieving triumph, it becomes a determinant of public attitudes and may even be a stimulus to action. Plato treats the ridicule of Socrates in Aristophanes' *Clouds* as playing a great part in the formation of the hostile feeling to which Socrates in the end fell victim. As we saw in the quotation from *Acharnians* above, the comic poet was willing to exploit the notion, in keeping with the tradition of didactic poetry (cf. p. 35), that it was his business to chastise the community by 'vilification' and so to repair its follies. The political message of some (not all) of Aristophanes' plays admits of concise summary: *Acharnians* and *Lysistrata* say 'Stop the war!' (*Peace* gives the appearance of saying this, but in fact the decision to make peace had already been taken some months before the play was put on). Understandably, some critics in recent times have treated such plays as passionate attempts by a poet of conservative sentiment to convert the audience to his own way of thinking on issues of policy and artistic taste. Others, observing that all the comic poets of Aristophanes' time and the generation before him seem from the surviving citations and fragments to have followed the same line, have regarded comedy as an art-form practised and favoured by one portion of the community to the discomfiture of the other portion. It has been suggested as another possibility that Aristophanic satire and vilification are the kind of fun which is tolerated on a privileged occasion by its victims as much as by the audience.

This last view is hard to sustain in the face of the fact that the Athenians did from time to time kill, outlaw, or otherwise penalize not only men who had failed them in the exercise of high office but also individuals suspected of religious offences, and the further fact that the Greeks in general, sensitive to shame, tended to regard public mockery as expressing and generating enmity (certain evidence shows that on more than one occasion there was short-lived legislation against personal attacks on stage). On the other hand, the 'message' of a play of Aristophanes becomes elusive when we try to define it in precise terms and draw a practical conclusion from it, and not least because of the absence of restraint in his use of fantasy, magic, and the supernatural. The Athenian farmer in *Peace* flies up to the abode of the gods on a dung-beetle which he has fattened to an enormous size, eludes War (who is pounding the cities of Greece in a mortar), summons men with ropes and picks from all over the Greek world to help him pull Peace up out of the cavern in which War has imprisoned her, and brings her back to earth. How his helpers get into the sky and back again is a mechanical question we are not allowed to ask. In *Birds* an Athenian citizen and his friend emigrate to the world of the birds, persuade them to build a fortified city somewhere, somehow, in the air between gods and men and force the gods to come to terms, so that the enterprising Athenian marries Queen, the 'housekeeper' of the gods, and becomes ruler of the universe. This is the world of fairy-tale, and it is not irrelevant to plays in which the sequence of events depends ostensibly on human action. In *Lysistrata,* for example, Aristophanes portrays the women of the belligerent cities as conspiring to go on strike against their husbands and swearing that they will not consent to sexual intercourse until the war has ended with a negotiated peace. The scene of the negotiations, however, disregards what would actually have been at issue at that date and portrays both sides as ready to concede everything as the price of resumption of sexual activity. A beautiful personification of Reconciliation is the focus of their interest.

LYSISTRATA (*to the Spartans*) ... And there was a time when the Messenians were pressing you hard, and Poseidon too made the earth quake. Then Cimon came with four thousand troops and saved all Sparta. That is how you were treated by the Athenians; yet you ravage our land, when we were your benefactors.

ATHENIAN (*triumphantly, indignantly*) They're in the wrong, Lysistrata!

SPARTAN (*perfunctorily*) We're in the wrong. (*Patting Reconciliation*) But what a fantastic arse!

(Aristophanes, *Lysistrata* 1141–8)

A play like *Lysistrata* transports the audience temporarily from the real world into fantasy, encouraging us to imagine how our troubles could be solved if the facts with which we have to cope were different from what we know them to be.

A simple, comprehensive theory which attempts to explain why we laugh is much harder to sustain than a theoretical explanation, at the same level of simplicity and comprehensiveness, of why we weep, and theories of comedy have so far proved as unsatisfactory as theories of laughter. To do justice to the data, generalizations about Aristophanic comedy need to be tentative and untidy. Listing of his types of humour is more helpful than theorizing, and the list must include abundant literary parody, personal and social satire, and many kinds of ingenious verbal play. Some other items may be (tentatively) grouped together in the category 'release from inhibition' and brought into relation with the element of reckless fantasy described above. Release is most obvious, at a superficial level, in the abundant use of vulgar anatomical and physiological terms which are entirely absent from epic, tragedy, and prose and occur outside comedy only in graffiti and in certain restricted genres of humorous poetry (cf. p. 34). The comic 'hero' — the character, that is to say, who in one type of play triumphs at the end by ingenuity, resilience, and noisy bullying — is apt to be earthy, philistine, cynical, and disillusioned, always prompt to treat poets and intellectuals as pretentious and civil and military officers as corrupt and self-seeking. The chorus too may voice the ordinary citizen's natural resentment towards his superiors:

. . . instead of looking up to some bloody colonel with three crests on his helmet and a dazzling cloak. A Lydian dye, he says it is — but if he ever has to go into battle with that cloak, he's dyed himself, good and brown. Then he's the first to run away, wagging his crests like a blue-nosed ostrich, and I'm left standing there in goal. And when they've come home, it's diabolical what they do, putting some of us on the lists, crossing out others, two or three times over. 'Expedition tomorrow!' But no food bought, of course; he didn't know he was going to be on an expedition. He just goes and looks at the list by the statue of Pandion and sees his own name on it. What a mess! He doesn't know what to do, and runs around looking sour. That's how they treat us countrymen — but not the townsmen, oh no! Yellow bastards!

(Aristophanes, *Peace* 1172–86)

The power of officers, administrators and politicians over the Athenian citizen was limited, but the power of the gods over mankind is unlimited, and the performance of comedy at the dramatic festivals was an occasion on which the Athenians could hit back by subjecting the gods and goddesses themselves to ridicule. The hero of *Birds* greatly enjoys himself in humiliating and bamboozling the gods who come to negotiate peace. The spokesman of the delegation is Poseidon, and he is accompanied by Herakles — a greedy and simple-minded brute — and a Thracian god whose Greek is very limited.

POSEIDON (*to the Thracian god*) What *are* you doing? You've got your cloak over your left shoulder! Now, put it the other way, over your right . . . Stand *still*! Hell! You're the most barbarous god I've ever seen, by a long way. (*To Herakles*) Now, Herakles: what are we going to do?
HERAKLES You've heard my opinion already. Choke the life out of the man, whoever he is, this man who's cut off the gods with his wall.
POSEIDON (*patiently*) But now, look, Herakles: we've been elected as envoys, to have *peace* talks.
HERAKLES Choke him twice as hard, then, that's what I say.

(Aristophanes, *Birds* 1567ff., 1572–8)

This play was produced at just the time when the Athenians were trying to catch and kill men whom they believed guilty of mutilating statues of Hermes and parodying the Eleusinian Mysteries at a private party. The Athens of Aristophanes was 'pluralistic' in the sense that it accommodated not only within itself every shade of religious opinion, from the bigoted or naïve to the sophisticated and sceptical, but also in the sense that the average individual found it possible to satisfy contradictory emotional needs on different occasions, one day seeking the goodwill of the gods by piety and sacrifice, the next day relieving his feelings by ridicule of the supernatural rulers of his existence.

In *Women at the Thesmophoria* ('Thesmophoriazusae'), produced in 411, and *Frogs,* produced in 405 (a few months before the disastrous sea-battle which ended the Peloponnesian War in favour of Athens' enemies). Aristophanes exploits the theme of tragic poetry. The former play contains much parody of Agathon and Euripides. In the latter, Dionysus, the god in whose honour the dramatic festivals were held, goes down to the underworld to bring Euripides back to earth. After an adventurous journey, which involves him in some absurd and humiliating predicaments and at the same time demonstrates the toughness and resourcefulness of· his slave, he finds the ghost of Euripides wrangling with the ghost of Aeschylus (who died fifty years earlier) over entitlement to the 'throne of poetry' in the underworld. He stages a contest between them, and in the end decides to bring back not Euripides but Aeschylus. The criteria he adopts, which by implication the audience is invited to adopt, strike many critics as naïve, starting from the premise that the tragic poet's function is to make the citizenry morally better and proceeding to judge individual plays, scenes, and passages of Aeschylus and Euripides by their theatrical effect and poetic style. The play offers us no encouragement to admire Aeschylus as a thinker; indeed, the last chorus, contrasting 'chattering with Socrates' with 'what matters in the art of tragedy', suggests that tragedy in Euripides' hands has become tepid through intellectualization. The contest between the two ghosts affords Aristophanes the occasion for some acute parody of their styles, as in this pseudo-Euripidean monody, in which the heroine, awakened by a terrifying dream, discovers that her neighbour has stolen the cockerel from her chicken-run.

> Ah, deity of the waves!
> This is it!
> Ah, neighbours,
> look upon these monstrosities!
>
> *
>
> I — unhappy! — was intent upon my tasks,
> whirr-lllinnng in my hands
> the spindle, laden with flax.
>
> *

And up he flew, flew, into the sky
on lightest point of wing,
and to me he left woes, woes;
and tears, tears from my eyes
I cast, I cast — miserable!

(Aristophanes, Frogs 1341ff., 1356–8, 1352–5)

No works of Aristophanes have survived from the years immediately after Athens' defeat and humiliation, but towards the last years of his life he adopted, and may well have pioneered, a new trend in comedy, exemplified by *Assembly of Women* ('Ecclesiazusae') and *Wealth* ('Plutus', datable to 388). Both these plays have themes which, with small adjustments, would fit the circumstances of many Greek states at most times. In the former the women disguise themselves as men, pack the assembly at dawn, and pass laws which turn the structure of society upside-down, transferring sexual initiative to women and abolishing private property. In *Wealth* a citizen discovers the god Wealth himself and cures him of his blindness, thus acquiring unlimited wealth for his own family and the power to ensure that correlation between prosperity and merit whose normal absence is asserted by the Greek saying 'Wealth is blind'. The general moral character of the play and its detachment from Athenian topicalities and personalities, together with its comparative lack of obscenity, ensured that it was read in late antiquity and at Byzantium more than any other comedy. Its most remarkable theatrical feature is its perfunctory treatment of the chorus, which is composed of the lucky citizen's neighbours. After one passage of dialogue and song from them early in the play, we have only bare indications in the text that at certain breaks in the action the chorus sang and danced, but the songs are not there and presumably were not composed by the poet himself. This development is foreshadowed in the second half of *Assembly of Women*.

III

By contrast with tragedy, which seems increasingly to have lost confidence during the fourth century B.C., treating the great tragic poets of the preceding century as unsurpassable masters, the development of comedy was not retarded by adherence to tradition. After the death of Aristophanes its formal features continued to change in the direction indicated by his last plays, particularly in the severance of the chorus from the plot and their relegation to musical interludes, and many prolific and inventive dramatists experimented with new motifs and themes. Hundreds of citations from fourth-century comedies are preserved in the surviving works of later authors, including anthologists, but citations naturally fail to tell us what we would most like to know: the architecture, plots, and overall effect of the plays from which they are drawn. For the last quarter of the century, together with the earlier part of the third century, we have always been better informed, thanks to the Latin adaptations of Greek comedies of that period by the Roman comic poets Plautus and Terence; and during the last seventy years the discovery of fragmentary Greek texts of Menander has given us direct knowledge of much that had previously been a matter of inference. Menander, who produced his first plays some two generations after the death of Aristophanes and wrote more than a hundred before he died, middle-aged, in 292, came to be regarded as the supreme poet of 'New Comedy' as Aristophanes was of 'Old Comedy'. We have one of his plays, *Dyskolos* ('The Bad-Tempered Man'), virtually complete; very large portions of a further five are continuously readable, and new fragments continue to be published.

A distinctive feature of the plots of New Comedy is the conflict and suffering generated, particularly between parent and child, lovers, or married couples, by ignorance and error. A father believes that his concubine was seduced in his absence by his adopted son and that the baby in her custody is the result; he is right in thinking that his adopted son begot the baby, but its mother is actually the neighbour's unmarried daughter. A soldier learns that his concubine has been observed in affectionate conversation with a youth; enraged, he cuts off her hair, not knowing that the youth is her brother. The identity of a baby exposed at birth and rescued by someone unknown to its parents is revealed at last by tokens abandoned with it. Such motifs are akin to the 'recognition' motif in tragedy, to which Aristotle's *Poetics* attaches importance, but there are some distinctions to be drawn. The revelation of an individual's identity in tragedy may on occasion constitute a 'happy ending' (Ion and Creusa in Euripides' *Ion*), but it may also create a situation from which the plot proceeds to develop into an exciting adventure (Orestes and Iphigenia in Euripides' *Iphigenia in Tauris*) or into sombre and disturbing events (Orestes and Electra in Aeschylus' and Euripides' treatment of the story). It may indeed, as in the case of Oedipus's recognition of his own identity, plunge us into horrors which we would have wished to see averted. In New Comedy mutual recognition and the dissipation of error always contribute to ending the sufferings and frustrations of sympathetic characters, and the audience has the assurance from the first moment of the play that good will win and evil be defeated. The dramatist plays effectively upon our sensibility, but we do not leave the theatre saddened by the irreversible cruelty of fate.

The influence of tragedy upon New Comedy is most obvious in Menander's use of a prologue-speaker whose function — we may compare Hermes in Euripides' *Ion* or Aphrodite in his *Hippolytus* — is to explain the situation to us and, on occasion, hint at what is to come. This speaker is as a rule divine, and relevant to the action of the play, but not a participant seen, heard, or addressed by the other participants. In Menander's *Dyskolos* the prologue is spoken by Pan, whose shrine (shared with the Nymphs) is represented by one of the three doors at the back of the stage-area; he claims to be rewarding the piety of the old farmer's daughter by making a rich young man fall in love with her at first sight. In other plays Menander begins with a scene which arouses the audience's interest, and only then brings on a divine person, for example, Fortune or Misapprehension, to answer some of the questions which the scene has provoked in us, rather as Aristophanes sometimes makes a character in the first scene of a play turn to the audience and explain the grotesque situation into which he has launched us without warning.

Although a New Comedy play may posit providential design or the arbitrary act of a supernatural being as the mainspring of the plot, it avoids the portrayal of events which absolutely demand a supernatural explanation; from the observer's point of view, after all, 'a god, it seems, made me fall in love with her' and 'I suddenly fell in love with her' are alternative descriptions of the

same event. The casual mingling of mortals, deities, and personified abstractions which so often occurs in Old Comedy is absent
from New Comedy; so is Old Comedy's cheerful disregard of the
constraints imposed by physical cause and effect in time and
space and by social realities in the interaction between the
resourceful comic hero and the adversaries whom he must
overcome. The unrealistic elements of New Comedy lie in its
lavish use of remarkable coincidence, a feature inevitable in a
genre which exploits the drama of recognition, and the speed with
which characters change their minds, no less inevitable when a
play has to create and then resolve a tangle of events within the
compass of a thousand verses. By a moralizing speech about the
uses of wealth the young man in *Dyskolos* persuades his father to
accept what he rejected a few minutes before, a poor but
admirable young farmer as son-in-law. 'You don't need to
moralize to me!' says the father, half affectionate, half grumbling,
and his words make us take the son's speech in retrospect more as
a revelation of character than as a stilted convention.

It is in fact in characterization and the nuances of social
interaction that Menander displays his genius, rather than in the
moralizing dicta which made him a rich seam for anthologists to
mine. An element of 'stock' characterization — perhaps 'predictable' characterization is a better term — is apparent from time to
time, especially in the portrayal of garrulous and self-important
cooks (cooking, incidentally, was a male trade). Yet on the whole
the temptation presented to the prolific dramatist by recurrent
roles — irascible fathers, spirited but warm-hearted young
women, resourceful slaves who rescue their ingenuous young
owners from hopeless predicaments — is resisted, and what
might have been stereotypes are turned into individuals. Two
passages will convey something of the flavour of Menander. In
the first, from *Epitrepontes* ('Men going to arbitration'), a slave,
Onesimus, treats with bland and confident irony the father-in-
law (Smicrines) of his master.

ONESIMUS Who's that knocking at the door? Ah! It's Smicrines! A hard
man! He's come for the dowry and his daughter.
SMICRINES Yes, I have, God damn you!
ONESIMUS Well, you're absolutely right. It's a credit to your brains and

your good sense that you're getting on with it. The way the dowry's gone
— it's *shocking*!

SMICRINES For Heaven's sake —

ONESIMUS Do you think that the gods have got time, Smicrines, to
allocate good and ill to each individual day by day?

SMICRINES What are you talking about?

ONESIMUS I'll explain. In the world there are, give or take a few, a
thousand cities, and thirty thousand people living in each one. Do the
gods ruin or save every separate one of those men?

SMICRINES (*despite himself, arrested by the idea*) How could they? Their lives
would be pretty busy!

ONESIMUS Well, are you going to say 'So the gods don't care about us'?
In every man they've put a captain of his soul — his character. It's
inside, and it destroys us if we treat it wrongly, but it can keep us right
too. That's our god, and it's his doing that each of us succeeds or fails.
You'll propitiate *him* by not doing anything wrong or stupid — then
you'll succeed.

SMICRINES You thug, you mean *my* character's doing something stupid
now?

ONESIMUS It's killing you.

SMICRINES (*enraged*) *Insolence*!

(Menander, *Epitrepontes* 1078–101)

In the second passage, from *Perikeiromene* ('Woman who gets her
hair shorn off'), a soldier, Polemon, reacts with pathetic despair
to desertion by the concubine he has maltreated.

POLEMON *I*'ve thought of her as my *wife*.

PATAECUS Don't get so excited! Who gave her in marriage?

POLEMON Who gave her to *me*? Why, *she* did!

PATAECUS Well, fine, maybe she liked you, and now she doesn't, and
she's gone off because you didn't treat her the right way.

POLEMAN Not the right way? What do you mean? To hear you say that
— that's the cruellest blow of all!

PATAECUS (*soothingly*) You're in love, I can see that perfectly well. That's
why what you're doing now is *crazy* . . .

*

POLEMON I don't know what to say — except — I'll hang myself
Glycera's left me! She's *left* me, Pataecus — *Glycera*! If you agree to do it
— after all, you knew her, and you've often spoken with her — go and
talk to her, be a go-between for me, *please*!

PATAECUS Yes, yes, I'll do that.

POLEMON And I'm sure you must be a good speaker.

PATAECUS Well, not too bad.

POLEMON You *must* do it, Pataecus! It's the only way out of all this. If I've *ever* hurt her in any way — if I don't do my best, all the time, in everything — Now, if you had a look at her clothes and jewels —

PATAECUS No, really, it's not necessary.

POLEMON *Do* look at them, Pataecus, *please*! It'll make you more sorry for me.

PATAECUS Oh, Lord!

POLEMON Come on! What dresses! And when she's put one of them on, what a wonderful sight! Maybe you hadn't seen her in them.

PATAECUS Yes, I have.

POLEMON And she was so tall, really, it was marvellous. Oh, what's the point now of saying how tall she was? Nattering on like this, I must be going out of my mind.

PATAECUS No, no, not a bit.

(Menander, *Perikeiromene* 489–95, 504–24)

Old Comedy, for all the brutal directness of its appeal, proved ephemeral: it was too closely tied to the issues which preoccupied one city-state at one period of time, and the standpoint of its humour was too often naïve and philistine. New Comedy, designed to please an audience of more refined perceptions and more inhibited imagination, spread over the Mediterranean world in the wake of tragedy; its appeal was wide, and its adaptation to Roman tastes by Terence made it an enduring influence in the West. It is an irony of history that the survival of Aristophanes in the Eastern Mediterranean, where Menander did not survive to the end of the Middle Ages, may have owed more to the interest which fifth-century Athens and pure Attic usage held for scholars and historians than to their appreciation of Aristophanes' work as comic drama. In East and West alike, 'Middle' Comedy, which transformed the Old into the profoundly different New, was destined to perish.

6   The classical historians

In ancient Egypt and other civilizations of the Near East it was the immemorial practice of kings to set up inscriptions giving detailed and systematic narratives of their own achievements in war, administration, and public works: boastful in tone and no doubt often false, but none the less a frame of reference for the historical consciousness of those who could read, and admitting of transcription and circulation on papyrus or baked clay. By contrast, if a Greek in (say) 500 B.C. wanted to learn about the past history of his own city-state, he could not look it up. No historical writings were available to him, no archives, no chroni-cles; only (in some states) a bare list of the holders of annual magistracies or priesthoods and texts of laws, usually undated. Epic poetry purported to tell him about the remoter past, the heroic age, but it was rich in contradictions, and it was possible to argue from motives of patriotism for or against the genuineness of passages of epic. Some narrative poems about a particular city or area described or mentioned events of more recent date, but these were not numerous. Historical curiosity aroused by what one had seen or heard — 'When was this temple built?', 'On this statue in the sanctuary it says "Dedicated by Euthydicus", but who was Euthydicus?', or 'Who was the wealthy king Gyges to whom this poem of Archilochus makes an allusion?' — could not be satisfied by the objects or texts which provoked it, but only by asking people who were interested in such things and had been told about them by other people of the previous generation. Answers to 'Who . . .?' and 'When . . .?' might be given in genealogical terms, for prominent Greek families were interested in their own genealogies and their putative links with the heroes of legend; and such answers are convertible, by rule of thumb, into 'about *n* years ago'. Or an answer might sometimes be given (truly or falsely) in terms of the chronological scale of the city concerned, e.g. 'in the archonship of Amphitimus', and if a complete list existed that answer was convertible into 'n years ago'. For the colour and substance of narrative history the inquirer was essentially dependent on oral tradition, the narrative ingredient of conversation, unsystematic, often morally or politically tendentious, constituting a stock from which obsolete items tend to be shed as newer material is fed in.

In the early fifth century the characteristic Greek curiosity which had already addressed itself to the constitution and working of the world of nature was turned on to the human past. 'History', however, strictly defined as the study of what human beings have done and said and thought, did not at once separate itself from geography, natural history, and myth, or from the scientific and religious speculation to which these topics gave rise. Such interests are conspicuous in Herodotus, the earliest Greek historian whose work we possess. He came from Halicarnassus, a city of Dorian origin on the coast of Asia Minor, but he wrote in the Ionic dialect, which had become widely accepted as the appropriate medium for prose exposition. Some clear allusions in the last four of the nine 'books' into which his work is divided indicate that he finished writing after (perhaps very soon after) 430. How long he had taken to draft, compose and revise his work as a whole is not known. He presents the story of a massive complex of events, the conflict between the Greeks and the Persian Empire, which began when the Persians reached the Aegean in the 540s, after conquering Lydia, and reached its climax in the defeat of the Persian invasion of Greece (480–479) and in the immediately consequent liberation of the Greeks of the islands and the Aegean coasts of Asia Minor. Herodotus views his theme as a conflict of Europe and Asia, and thus begins with the rise of the kingdom of Lydia in the seventh century B.C. Croesus, the last king of Lydia, earned himself an important place in Greek tradition by making lavish gifts to the oracle at Delphi and consulting it before launching the imprudent attack on Persia which brought about his own overthrow. The story of Croesus is the main strand running through book i of Herodotus; it is not until the last third of book vi that we reach the first (limited) Persian attack on the Greek mainland, and books vii–ix are devoted to Xerxes' invasion of Greece.

In his opening sentence Herodotus describes his work as the exposition of the results of his own *historiē*, 'enquiry', and his purpose is:

. . . that what has been done may not fade in time from the memory of man, and great and remarkable achievements, whether of Greeks or of foreign (*barbaroi*) peoples, may not lack the honour of remembrance.

His readiness to credit foreign nations with 'great . . . achievements', and his equal readiness to enrich his tale of 'achievements' with a wealth of curious and interesting data of all kinds, show us what picture of the world was entertained by a gifted and articulate Greek of the early classical period. His willingness to display his own thoughts and feelings in comment on his material makes him a person — an intensely Greek person — whom we feel we have come to know by the time that we have finished a first reading. All Greek historians down to 400 B.C. can fairly be regarded as pioneers, the creators of historiography, prompt to experiment, and we must not lose sight of that fact if we are ever inclined to criticize Herodotus for his discursiveness, his lack of historiographical system, and his frequent indifference to our demand for clarification of the time-relation between sequences of events narrated in widely separated contexts. Since he twice refers forward to an account of Assyrian history which is not in fact to be found in his work as we have it, it may be that had he lived longer he would have made the work even more discursive, by incorporating many chapters on Assyria — or less so, by putting much of his material on the geography and early history of Asia and Africa into separate works. To judge from book ii, the former is the more likely alternative. He begins that book with the statement that the Persian king Cambyses, son of Cyrus, campaigned against Egypt. The story is not resumed until iii 1, 'against this [sc. king of Egypt] Amasis Cambyses took the field', for immediately after ii 1 he has much to say about the antiquity of Egyptian civilization and the physical boundaries and features of Egypt, with a discussion of the source of the Nile and the cause of its summer flood (he acknowledges, but unfortunately rejects, the hypothesis that it is fed by melting snow). Then he announces an even longer excursus:

I am going to give an extended account of Egypt, because it has a greater number of remarkable things in it, and presents us with a greater number of extraordinary works, than any other country; for that reason I shall say more about it.

(Herodotus ii 35.1)

There follow: the social and religious practices of the Egyptians, the wild life of Egypt (interspersed with further information on customs and religion), and, finally, approximately one half of the book, a history of Egypt from the earliest times down to Amasis, enlivened by a digression on the myth of Helen's stay in Egypt.

Whether Herodotus drew to any significant extent on written sources is doubtful. He could certainly draw on one earlier writer, Hecataeus of Miletus, whom he mentions by name, for geographical and genealogical data, and perhaps also for material relating to the foundation of colonies; but we know so little about the nature and content of the work of the earliest Greek historical writers, and there is so large a margin of uncertainty about their dates, that the extent of Herodotus' dependence on them cannot be assessed. The question of his sources for the history of Egypt and Asia is more positively challenging. He speaks of visiting Tyre and several places in Egypt, and claims to have been told much by Egyptian priests, but our credulity is put under strain when these priests expound Greek mythology in Greek terms. It has already been strained, at the very outset of his work, by the statement that 'those Persians who are learned in tradition' attribute the origin of the conflict between Europe and Asia to the seizure of Io, daughter of Inachus, king of Argos, by Phoenician sailors. And one of his most implausible scenes, a debate between Persian nobles in 521 on whether the Persian Empire should remain a monarchy or become an oligarchy or a democracy (a debate charged throughout with familiar Greek sentiments on the merits and demerits of the three rival systems), is introduced with the words: 'A discussion was held which some Greeks find hard to believe; but it *was* held.' (Herodotus iii 80.1). Modern opinions on Herodotus' oriental sources range from a trustfulness which admits regretfully that he made some bad mistakes (as indeed he did, on any reckoning) to a dismissal of his entire work as artful and systematic fiction. It is possible that his direct informants were Greeks or Greek-speakers whose reliability and understanding he greatly overestimated and whose statements, already distorted by assimilation to Greek motifs, he distorted even further by his own interpretations of them.

Be that as it may, the constituent of his work which deals with the history of the Greeks is ostensibly a synthesis of the traditions, increasingly detailed as we progress from 540 to 479, existing in the third quarter of the fifth century B.C. Herodotus not infrequently abstains from decision between alternative traditions, though willing to tip the scales one way or the other, as in:

The Spartans say that when the bowl was being taken to Sardis it passed through Samian waters and the Samians, hearing of it, attacked with warships and confiscated it. But the Samians themselves say that when the Spartans who were conveying the bowl were too late, and heard that Sardis and Croesus had been taken, they sold the bowl at Samos, and some private individuals there bought it and dedicated it in the sanctuary of Hera. Perhaps those who sold it said, when they came back to Sparta, that they had been robbed of it by the Samians.

(Herodotus i 70.3)

When the Samians who had been driven out by Polycrates came to Sparta ... Then the Spartans mounted an expedition to Samos; according to the Samians, they were repaying a debt of friendship, because the Samians themselves had earlier helped Sparta with a fleet against the Messenians, but according to the Spartans, they sent the expedition because they wished not so much to answer a Samian request for help as to punish Samos for the theft of the bowl which they sent to Croesus and of the breastplate which Amasis the king of Egypt had sent to Sparta as a gift. For the Samians seized the breastplate the year before the bowl ...

(Herodotus iii 46.1–47.2)

After recounting in detail current allegations that Argos had been in treacherous negotiations with Xerxes before the Persian invasion, he adds: 'I have an obligation to tell what is told, but I am under no obligation at all to believe it; and that is to be taken as valid for everything I tell.' (Herodotus vii 152.3) We, his readers, are under no obligation to believe or disbelieve, but only (if we are historians) to consider which, among all the data which he offers us, combine with independent evidence to make coherent historical hypotheses. Naturally, within a complex of traditions relating to a period for which archaeological and archival documentation is scanty, only a small fraction of the detail enters into such combinations. We do not as a rule have grounds for deciding whether Herodotus reported tradition accurately or how much he rejected in choosing what to report.

Tradition tends to express the location of events in time in genealogical terms, and this accounts for much of the difficulty we encounter when we try to fit Herodotus' material into a single chronological scheme. He stands, however, at a point of transition in historiography, for it may well be the application of a formula accepted by him as valid (three generations = a hundred years) which underlies his polemical assertion that 'Homer and Hesiod lived four hundred years ago, and no earlier'. A further assumption must underlie his statements about the lengths of reign of the kings of Lydia from Gyges to Croesus, for a cross-check with Assyrian records shows that he was badly mistaken about the date of Gyges. Earlier fifth-century writers on genealogy interested themselves in the heroic age, and Herodotus has no hesitation in setting out in detail the descent of the Spartan kings from Herakles. Elsewhere, however, he draws a distinction of the greatest importance:

Polycrates is the first Greek known to us who had the ambition to rule the sea — apart from Minos of Cnossus or anyone before Minos who ruled the sea; but in what are called *human* times Polycrates was the first.

(Herodotus iii 122.2)

Taking it for granted that Helen, Paris, and Priam actually existed, Herodotus nevertheless adopts the view, which he attributes to 'the Egyptian priests' (he does not mention Stesichorus [p. 53]), that Helen spent the Trojan War safely in Egypt, not at Troy; thus he rejects a central element of the *Iliad* as fiction ('for Priam and his family would not have been so insane . . .'), but does not take this scepticism about legend to the logical conclusion which lies within his grasp, namely that the Trojan War itself may be a fictitious event. The narrative of epic poetry abounds in dialogue, and so do folk-tales, political gossip, and the anecdotes embedded in our ordinary conversation ('So he said, "What's all this, then?", he said . . .'). It would not have occurred to Herodotus to eliminate this element from historical narrative; and, belonging as he did to a culture which enjoyed oratory as an art-form and was accustomed to the taking of political and military decisions under the immediate impact of persuasive speech, he cast his accounts of deliberation into direct speech, as, for example, in this description of the Greek commanders arguing before the battle of Salamis:

When Themistocles spoke, the Corinthian commander Adimantus, son of Ocytus, said, 'Themistocles, in the games the competitors who start too soon get whipped.' Themistocles replied, 'Yes, but those who are left behind get no prizes.' On this occasion his reply to the Corinthian was mild. And to Eurybiades he said nothing now of what he had said before, to the effect that as soon as the Greeks moved from Salamis they would flee this way and that, because it would have been most unseemly for him to accuse the allies in their presence. He kept to a different argument, saying, 'Now it lies with *you* to save Greece by staying and fighting a sea-battle *here,* as I say we should, and not doing as *they* say, moving the fleet over to the Isthmus . . .'

(Herodotus viii 60 α)

The more extensive speeches which Herodotus puts into the mouths of his characters can be regarded as belonging to a very old tradition, if we recall the assembly-scene in the second book of the *Iliad,* but they also established a technique to which later Greek historians adhered with varying degrees of fidelity to evidence or preoccupation with rhetoric.

II

Just at the time when Herodotus was finishing his work, the Athenian Thucydides was embarking on history of a very different kind. Thucydides was a grown man, perhaps already in his forties, when the Peloponnesian War broke out in 431. It was a conflict, foreseeable and foreseen, between Athens and her Aegean empire on the one hand and Sparta and her allies (collectively, 'the Peloponnesians') on the other, and Thucydides at once conceived an ambition to write its history. He held a high military command in 424, but went into exile when he failed to save a place to which the Athenians attached great importance; during his exile he spent some time on the other side, returning to Athens only in 404/3, after the war had ended in Athens' decisive defeat. Although he refers more than once to the end of the war and its total duration, his account of it breaks off abruptly with events of the winter of 411/10. The whole work is consistent in style, but not in historiographical technique, and in particular his account of 412–411 gives the impression that that portion was not revised to the standard he set himself elsewhere.

When we turn from Herodotus to Thucydides, we are likely to be struck more by the differences than by the similarities, but some of these differences are essentially linguistic and others (including some of the profoundest) are due less to disparity of intellectual stature or artistic purpose than to a fundamental contrast between their subjects. Dealing with events which took place never less than thirty years before his own maturity as a writer, and often a hundred or more years before, Herodotus was normally dependent on oral tradition, and he was aware of its deficiencies and limitations. Thucydides, writing the history of a war which fell entirely within his own adult lifetime, was present on some of the occasions which he describes, and he derived his information on the rest from participants who could be interrogated to an extent impossible in dealing with those who simply transmitted what they had been told by a previous generation. One consequence is that Thucydides was able to expound the events of the Peloponnesian War in strict order, year by year, dividing each year into 'summer', within which most major operations were undertaken, and 'winter', when operations were usually limited. A second and more important consequence is that, perhaps through his awareness of the scale of the evidence available to him and of its difference in kind from inherited tradition, he did not judge it appropriate in serving up the banquet to tell us the recipe or the source of the ingredients. So rarely does he reveal any trace of contradictions within the evidence available, or confess inability to fill a gap, or hesitate in the attribution of motive or intention, that we cannot form an opinion of our own on the adequacy of his methods of research or the soundness of his judgement.

He is unquestionably a magisterial writer, equally gifted in the vivid portrayal of conflict and suffering and in persuasive and memorable generalization about the constants of human history. His narrative is often cool, restrained, and precise, but he has a sharp sense of climax, illustrated in the following two extracts.

The first concerns the fate of the Theban force which tried to take over Plataea in the spring of 431, and the second the Athenian prisoners kept in the quarries at Syracuse after the defeat of the Athenian expedition against Syracuse in 413.

When the Thebans realized the trick that had been played on them, they went into close formation and resisted the Plataeans wherever they attacked. They repelled them two or three times; but then, when the Plataeans attacked with a great roar, and at the same time women and slaves, screaming and yelling, pelted them with stones and tiles from the houses, and heavy rain came on in the darkness, they panicked and turned and fled through the city, most of them not knowing, in the darkness and mud, which streets to take if they were to get out (for all this happened at the end of a moon), whereas they had pursuers who did know the way and could stop them escaping, so that the majority of them perished.

(Thucydides ii 4.2)

The place was deep and small, and many were crowded in it. At first the sunshine and continuing heat oppressed them, for there was no roof over them; and then the cold autumn nights came on, a change which generated sickness. Since they did everything in the same place, for lack of space, and also the corpses of those who died from wounds or through the change of climate or some such cause were heaped all together one on top of another, the stench was unbearable; and they were tormented moreover by hunger and thirst, for the Syracusans gave each man, for eight months, half a pint of water and a pint of grain a day. Of all the sufferings that it could be expected men cast into such a place would undergo, there was not one that did not afflict them.

(id. vii 87.1f.)

In reading Thucydides we are beset unremittingly by the temptation to accept him not simply as a great writer but also as a masterly historian, and his interpretation of the Peloponnesian War as definitive, but we must recognize temptation for what it is. He wished and liked to get things right, and in declaring his purpose he strikes a nice balance between confidence and modesty:

When an audience hears my work, the absence of a story-element in it will perhaps lessen their enjoyment; but if it is judged useful by those who want to get a clear picture both of events which have happened in the past and of events which, the human situation being what it is, will happen in the future in the same or comparable form, that will be enough. My work has been composed as a permanent possession, not as a prize-composition for a single hearing.

(id. i 22.4)

Yet half a page later he betrays, by a degree of self-confidence amounting to arrogance, a blind spot in his (and other ancient historians') concept of the historian's business: 'On their reasons for breaking the treaty, I have begun by setting out the charges and disputes, *so that no one need ever again investigate the cause of the outbreak of so great a Greek war*' (id. i 23.5). In our own time the causes of the Peloponnesian War have been repeatedly, and not unprofitably, re-examined; and if it is hard to say whether this re-examination has vindicated or invalidated Thucydides' view, the difficulty is largely due to disagreement on what his view actually is, since different passages in book i point in different directions. Perhaps he would have clarified the issue had he lived long enough to subject the book to further revision; perhaps, on the other hand, he thought — mistakenly — that he had already expressed himself clearly enough.

He is not easy to read in Greek; he exploited to the full the potential of the Greek language for abstract expression, he often tried to say a great deal in few words, and in this process he made some bold linguistic experiments which were not imitated by later writers. Unlike Herodotus, he offers us virtually no conversation-pieces, but in presenting a debate on an important political issue he puts extensive speeches into the mouth of one or more of the participants. For example, his account of the Athenian decision to send a major expedition against Syracuse in 415 opens with a speech by Nicias advocating the cancellation of the project, a speech by Alcibiades insisting on its execution, and a second speech by Nicias emphasizing the magnitude of the forces needed to bring it off successfully. When the news of the Athenian preparations reaches Syracuse, the Syracusan Hermocrates makes a speech warning his countrymen of the danger, while his political opponent Athenagoras plays it down. These speeches are not designed, as speeches in later historians were designed (after the pioneering phase of Greek historiography was over), to display the historian's ability to express in elegant terms the issues which seemed to him implicit in historical situations. They are there because Thucydides knew that oratory was of crucial importance to the taking of decisions by Greek cities, and plenty of information on what had been said on such occasions was available to him. The language of the speeches is his own, identical with that in which he analyses complex situations; it is more condensed, sophisticated, and obscure than the language of speeches actually addressed to mass audiences can ever have been, and it does not reflect the national dialects or (save in one short instance) the different cultural levels of the speakers. The difference between a Herodotean and a Thucydidean speech is illustrated by the following pair of examples: the first comes from the Persian Artabanus' advice to Xerxes, the second from Pericles' speech to the Athenians after the great plague of 430 had ravaged Athens.

You see that the god blasts those living things that rise above others, and does not permit them to vaunt themselves, but the small ones do not vex him at all; and you see that it is always against the highest buildings and trees of such a kind that he looses his shafts. For it is the way of the god to chastise all that rises above the rest. So too a great army is destroyed by a small one; it comes about that when the god in his jealousy inflicts panic or thunder upon them, they are destroyed, for all that they deserved better. For the god does not permit great ambitions to any but himself. The hastening of any undertaking begets errors, from which great losses are wont to come; but in holding back there are advantages, perhaps not apparent at the moment, but one may perceive them in time . . .

(Herodotus vii 10.6 ε)

For what is sudden and unexpected and most in conflict with previous calculation humbles the spirit; and that has happened to *you* through the plague, as much as anything, added to your other sufferings. Nevertheless, those who live in a great city and have been brought up in a way of life commensurate with it must be willing to withstand the greatest misfortunes and not allow the regard in which they are held to be diminished — for people think it equally just to blame anyone who through faint-heartedness falls short of his existing reputation and to detest him who in foolhardiness grasps at a reputation which is not his by right — but surmount their private distress and hold fast to the preservation of the common good.

(Thucydides ii 61.3f.)

The Herodotean passage uses the language of religion; only a minority of Thucydidean speakers ever do so, and Thucydides himself, though quite ready to acknowledge the part played in human affairs by religious belief, excludes the gods from his own exposition of historical cause and effect. In this respect his work is a major step forward in historiography, for historical discovery and explanation rest in the last resort on criteria of probability derived from generalization, which, in turn, is founded on observation. While we may entertain firm beliefs about the nature of the gods and the circumstances in which their intervention is to be welcomed or feared, we can hardly say what exactly would *probably* be done in pursuance of hidden purposes by divine beings often endowed with a degree of foreknowledge and inspired by inscrutable jealousies and favouritisms. It was very widely believed in Thucydides' time that the gods punish injustice, and very common to draw the conclusion that a sceptic acknowledges no moral restraints except those imposed by prudence in trying to escape detection and punishment. Similarly, confused thinking in our own time about the relation between religion and morality has generated an inclination to believe that Thucydides was an immoralist who respected only the successful exercise of power. Such a belief cannot survive confrontation with the chapters (iii 82ff.) in which he describes the increase in intensity of civil strife within Greek cities during the war and the cruelty, treachery, and dishonesty which in his view characterized it. In form a methodical analysis, these chapters are written throughout in the language of moral passion, evincing no trace of respect for mere success, and the values which the language reflects do not differ significantly from those of Herodotus' or Sophocles' characters — or indeed from ours. In general, however, Thucydides is reluctant to thrust his own moral and emotional responses upon his readers; plainly, he did not consider it a historian's duty to do so. The facts of the war suggested to him that people who were able to achieve the right balance of cool intelligence, energy, and resilient courage stood a much better chance of survival than those who trusted in the gods to defend righteous causes, and he shared in the Greek capacity to separate the perception and description of happenings from the observer's evaluative reaction to them.

He lived to see the total loss of the imperial power which his own city had exercised over the islands of the Aegean and its northern and eastern coasts. Athens had acquired great wealth by exacting tribute from others, disguising the threat of force as 'alliance', and justifying the use of force, sometimes merciless and vindictive in the punishment of rebellion, as defence of her vital interests. On more than one occasion her spokesmen are portrayed by Thucydides as realists who waste no time on the language of morality. The modern reader is apt to underrate the enthusiasm with which Athenians of all classes in the fifth century maintained the empire and in the fourth looked back on it with unrepentant pride; in fact, such anti-imperialist sentiment as there was came from extreme opponents of democracy. When the reader does realize this, he may fall into the opposite error of thinking that the Athenian democracy was actually more brutal than other Greek states in the exercise of power, and he expects Thucydides to take sides unambiguously on this issue. But the expectation is not met: Thucydides' own attitude to Athenian imperialism is a complicated question, to which much of interest is contributed by careful reading of his text and reflection on it, but it remains a question without a clear and simple answer.

III

Herodotus and Thucydides exemplified and reinforced a growing passion for historiography among intellectual Greeks in the Classical period. Some wrote chronicles, disposing in strict sequence the history of the Greek world (for example, Hellanicus, in the last part of the fifth century) or of Athens (Hellanicus again, and Androtion in the fourth century); others wrote more discursive history, in which unity of topic might, in varying degrees, take precedence over time-sequence (for example, Xenophon, Ephorus, and Theopompus, all in the fourth century). The many names we know may not be the whole story; one of the most interesting historical works surviving, a substantial portion of detailed narrative relating to the 390s, can still only be called, after the place where it was found, the *Hellenica of Oxyrhynchus*.

The unfinished state of Thucydides' account of the Peloponnesian War was a challenge to fourth-century historians, and among those who accepted the challenge and completed the story of the last seven years of the war was the Athenian Xenophon, the third of the only three Greek historians of the Classical period whose work has come down to us intact (one of the most influential of all, Ephorus, has not survived). Xenophon took service in the army of Greek mercenaries raised in 401 by Cyrus in rebellion against his brother, the king of Persia. When the rebellion was defeated, the principal Greek commanders murdered, and the mercenaries faced with the prospect of fighting their way through to safety, Xenophon was among the new commanders whom they elected, and he helped to bring them northwards through difficult and hostile country to the Black Sea. Once in contact again with the Greek world, now dominated by Sparta, Xenophon served under Spartan command, even against his native city, and as a traitor could not return to Athens. The Spartans gave him an estate in the north-western Peloponnese, where he lived until (in 371) Spartan power in the Peloponnese was broken by Thebes, and he took refuge at Corinth. The Theban threat brought Athens and Sparta together, and Xenophon was officially rehabilitated by the Athenians; we do not know whether he returned to Athens. He died soon after 356.

His activity as a writer was manifold: history, biography, moralizing and practical (even technical) essays, reminiscences of Socrates (cf. p. 110) as a moral teacher, dialogues, and a long work (*The Education of Cyrus*) which is not easily classified. His two major historical works are the *Anabasis* ('Journey to the Interior'), an account of the rebellion of Cyrus and the adventurous return of the Greek mercenaries, and the *Hellenica*, a history of the Greek mainland and the Aegean from the end of 411 (the point at which Thucydides broke off) to 362. Apart from the obvious fact that no book can have been completed at a date earlier than the latest historical event which it mentions, we have singularly little firm evidence for the order in which Xenophon's works were written; they may have been well spread over a forty-year period or largely concentrated in the last part of that period.

Throughout the *Anabasis*, which he originally put into circulation under a pseudonym, 'Themistogenes of Syracuse', Xenophon speaks of himself in the third person. In this narrative he appears as a man of exceptional fortitude, resilience, and resource, able to command, inspire, and persuade. Perhaps he was from the first such a man — he was, after all, chosen by the mercenaries. At any rate, the moral character and technical skills required of a successful leader are a topic in which he constantly reveals a deep interest. Men with such an interest are not always articulate, but Xenophon's readiness to put his observations and sentiments on paper sometimes verges on garrulity. In the teaching of Greek in western Europe during the last few centuries the *Anabasis* has played an important part, for Xenophon's narrative style is simpler than Thucydides', and we tend to think that descriptions of travelling and fighting in the past tense are more easily understood than political, moral, and philosophical argument in a greater variety of tenses. Those who read the work in translation, freed from preoccupation with the conjugation of Greek verbs, may well find that what they remember best from it is not the marches and the battles but the wealth of Greek attitudes and behavioural traits revealed by the lively and impassioned dialogues, exhortations, and reproofs which abound in it.

In the first part of the *Hellenica* (i 1.1–ii 3.10) Xenophon adopts a historiographical technique which approximates to Thucydides'; that is appropriate, since he is there completing the story of the Peloponnesian War. However, his imitation of his predecessor does not extend to a chronological precision which leaves us no room for argument, and some obscurities in the first chapter make it difficult to imagine (as has been suggested from time to time) that he inherited any kind of draft or notes from Thucydides. Once past the end of the Peloponnesian War, he plainly felt freer to organize his material as he wished, with no regard for the reader who likes to get everything in the right temporal order, and the imposition of such an order is made possible only by our use of the documentary inscriptions of the period and the survival, in abridgement and quotation by later writers, of other historical material from the fourth century. If we reconstruct the history of the first half of that century solely from datable Athenian inscriptions (the material from other states is comparatively scanty) we are struck above all by the energy and success with which the Athenians, after rapid recovery from crushing defeat, set about recreating a network of alliances throughout the Aegean. When we turn to the *Hellenica*, we may be surprised to find how little Xenophon reveals of that process — surprised, perhaps, because our view of Greek history in the classical period tends inevitably to be 'Athenocentric', and Xenophon looks at the first forty years of the fourth century from a different standpoint. For him the period begins with Spartan domination, the other major cities coalescing in alliance against Sparta, passes to Theban domination, which put Corinth and Athens into the Spartan camp, and ends with a vast but indecisive battle at Mantinea in 362. His last words are:

Although each side said that it had won, it was obvious that neither side had gained in territory, city, or dominion anything more than before the battle was fought. Confusion without decision was even greater, throughout Greece, after the battle than previously. This is the point at which my account ends; perhaps someone else will concern himself with subsequent events.

(Xenophon, *Hellenica* vii 5.27)

Unlike Thucydides, Xenophon freely allows his own religious convictions and moral reactions to colour his factual narrative, as in the following two passages. The first is taken from his account of a political massacre at Corinth on a festival day, the second from his zestful description of the disaster suffered by Corinth later in the same year (393).

When it was realized what was happening, the good citizens fled straightway, some to the statues of the gods in the market square and others to the altars. There their opponents, most unholy of men and (whether giving or taking the orders) with no vestige of respect for common usage in their hearts, slaughtered them in actual contact with the sacred objects, so that among those who were not themselves victims but were law-abiding people some were anguished in their hearts at the sight of such impiety.

(ibid. iv 4.3)

At this point those who got up the ladders jumped down from the wall and were killed; others perished jostling and fighting round the ladders, and others again were trampled and suffocated by one another. And the Spartans had no lack of enemies to kill, for on this occasion the god granted them the achievement of a victory beyond their wildest dreams; that a multitude of their enemies should be delivered into their hands, frightened, dismayed, exposing their unprotected side, no one turning to stand and fight but all totally offering themselves up for destruction — must that not be reckoned the work of a god?

(ibid. iv 4.12)

The Education of Cyrus purports to be a life of Cyrus I, ruler of the Persian Empire 549–529; it is in eight 'books', and takes its title from the first of the eight. A certain Ctesias, who had spent many years as a doctor of high repute at the Persian court, published in the early years of the fourth century a very extensive history of Persia; he claimed to have used Persian documents, and his work was certainly known to Xenophon. However, any expectation that for this reason *The Education of Cyrus* might prove a valuable source of information on the early history of Persia is quickly disappointed. It is in fact a historically reckless work, designed to display in its portrayal of Cyrus Xenophon's own ideal of monarchy and generalship; and its many authentically Persian details are contaminated with much that is Greek, particularly in respect of religious ideas and usage. Apart from medical and scientific works, it is probably less read today by students of Greek than any other major text which has survived from the archaic and classical periods, for its subject is remote from their interests, its long conversational passages are ponderous, and few share its author's preoccupation with cavalry training and tactics. Nevertheless, careful reading of this historical novel — as it is not altogether unfair to call it — gives us considerable insight into the mind of its author, a man who was in so many respects a typical Greek. He was eloquent, pious, and martial, born and bred in a democratic society and imbued with its frankness and directness in social intercourse, yet essentially authoritarian and paternalistic, proud of his own city even in exile, yet ready to pursue his own ambitions and interests wherever in the world an opportunity might present itself.

7 Classical science and philosophy

In the last few centuries the province of philosophy has been substantially reduced, since science has increasingly offered means, founded upon observation, calculation, and experiment, of answering questions to which at one time only a variety of purely speculative answers could be offered. We do not now ask a philosopher how the solar system originated or why certain plants do better in sandy soil, though we might invite his criticism of the reasoning and conceptual relations involved in scientific answers to those questions. Greeks of the archaic and classical periods whose curiosity was aroused by questions about the origin, constituents, and working of the universe did not have at their disposal, and could not readily envisage, those technical means of satisfying curiosity which our own civilization has developed. They inherited poetry (Hesiod's, for example) which narrated the origins of the universe in terms of personified entities, such as Earth, Sky, and Night, who mated and procreated, and they explained its mechanical regularities, notably the course of the Sun and the chain of phenomena dependent upon it, in terms of laws made by Zeus and obeyed by subordinate deities. The essential first step which was to lead both to scientific and to philosophical thought was taken when certain Greeks in the first half of the sixth century B.C. devised economical and comprehensive theories intended to explain the origin and the working of the universe by reference not to the actions of deities but to the properties of supposed 'basic elements' such as air, fire, water, and earth. The earliest thinkers known to have put written work into circulation are Anaximander and Anaximenes, both natives of Miletus; they wrote in prose, but the very scanty surviving quotations do not tell us anything about its literary quality.

The history of what we must for convenience's sake call

'philosophy' in the Greek world is essentially the history of a search for plausible explanations of ourselves and our environment at the highest possible level of generalization. In this search the boundaries of physics, chemistry, astronomy, biology, and psychology are indistinct; and since it was very hard to form theories in these fields without tackling, directly or by implication, beliefs about the existence, nature, and conduct of the gods, the boundaries between science, theology, ethics, and politics were readily crossed by a philosopher whose starting-point lay in one or other of those 'subjects'. Attention to the validity of particular arguments generated interest in the conditions of valid argument in general, and in the relation between deduction from first principles and induction from observation. This in due course resulted in very important Greek contributions to logic and the theory of knowledge. The construction of experiments played little part in Greek scientific thinking, and the application of science to technology was inconsiderable. But while philosophers explored metaphysical concepts, architects and masons put up great buildings, and musicians made and tuned instruments; people also succumbed to illness and injury, and doctors tried to cure them. Mensuration and music were activities in which mathematics had a part to play, and medicine one in which the interaction of practice, observation, and speculative theory found expression in written works.

On the majority of technical subjects the Greeks of the archaic and classical periods wrote no books. Medicine, however, is represented by a very large corpus of material, which raises — for the first time in this book — the question, 'What is literature?' It is possible, in compiling sets of instructions for dealing with fractures and dislocations, to write with such force and elegance that even a reader who has no knowledge of the subject and no wish or need to acquire such knowledge may experience a profound aesthetic satisfaction. It is also possible, in writing on any topic of practical concern only to doctors, to subsume the technical expositions under a general theory so comprehensive and comprehensible as to attract a wide range of non-specialist readers. There are Greek medical works which can be categorized as literature for either or both of those reasons, and many others whose claim to the status of literature is more doubtful. The name of Hippocrates is attached to all those that have been transmitted from the classical or early Hellenistic period; there were indeed medical works by other named writers, but we do not have them. Hippocrates of Cos was a distinguished doctor of the late fifth century, but it is far from certain that any single one of the texts attributed to him was actually his. The medical doctrines represented in the 'Hippocratic corpus', as the collection of texts is called, are varied and mutually inconsistent, and some doctrines attributed in other sources to Hippocrates himself are absent from the corpus. Among the medical works of general interest, *Environment* ('Airs, Waters and Places') and *Epilepsy* ('On the Sacred Disease') can safely be assigned to the fifth century B.C., and *The Origins of Medicine* ('On Ancient Medicine') may well be as early. *Epilepsy* is notable for its empirical — but by no means irreligious — approach to a phenomenon generally regarded as an arbitrary supernatural intervention. There is a great gulf between the medical literature which we have and the practices of which we hear in other literature, such as amulets, charms, spells, and visits to the sanctuary of Asclepius in the hope of miraculous cures. The gulf between medicine and philosophy is not so great, for the doctor, like any scientist, seeks theories whose value lies precisely in their generality and the scope of their application; yet the doctor, conscious of the role of practical experience in his *tekhnē* ('art' or 'skill'), must avoid a level of generality too rarified for application. The author of *The Origins of Medicine* insists on this:

All those who in attempting to speak or write about medicine have chosen a postulate (*hypothesis*) as the foundation of their argument — 'hot' or 'cold' or 'wet' or 'dry', or anything that they fancy — and so narrow down the fundamental cause of human sickness and death, postulating one or two things only, the same cause for all cases, . . . are obviously mistaken.

(Hippocrates, *The Origins of Medicine* 1)

Certain doctors and intellectuals (*sophistai*) say that it is impossible to understand medicine unless one knows what Man is, and that anyone who is going to treat patients rightly must learn that. Their argument, however, leads into philosophy, the way Empedocles and other writers on Nature have written on what Man fundamentally is.

(ibid. 20)

It was, however, philosophy, not the increasingly self-contained sciences, which was destined to occupy a central place in Greek prose literature — and was indeed already moving towards that central place by the time that the earliest surviving Greek scientific works were composed.

II

To the modern public the name of Socrates is probably better known than that of any other Greek. Yet Socrates himself (born in 470, executed in 399) put nothing at all into writing; in so far as his teaching and personality inspired portrayal of him by others (above all by Plato) he is a major figure in Greek literature, but his contribution to it is entirely indirect. The impetus he gave to philosophy in certain directions (while restricting it in others) and the originality and power of the 'Socratic dialogues' in which he is presented to the reader have combined to impose the label 'Presocratic' on all those Greek philosophical writers who preceded him, and on those of his contemporaries (or in some cases his juniors) who were philosophically free of his influence. We owe our knowledge of the Presocratics almost entirely to quotations and summaries in later writers; so far they are poorly represented among the papyrus fragments. The quotations suggest that down to the middle of the fifth century it was common for philosophical writers to claim unique insight and to treat predecessors, rivals, and public with undiscriminating contempt. This is especially noticeable among those who adhered to the older tradition of exposition in verse. Xenophanes dismissed as fiction the mass of inherited myth about conflicts in the supernatural world, blamed Homer and Hesiod for propagating morally debased notions of the gods, and attacked the prevailing adulation of athletic victors on the grounds that a wise man like himself is a much more useful member of the community than a champion boxer. Parmenides presented his doctrine of 'being' and 'not being' as divinely revealed to him alone, and regarded all other men as wallowing in helpless ignorance. Empedocles preached a doctrine of reincarnation, considered himself already to have become a god, and in one remarkable passage promises a disciple power to change the weather and resurrect the dead. The tradition which these poets represent may owe something to the exclusive and mystical character of the philosophical sect which Pythagoras founded in southern Italy in the late sixth century, and something also to the divine contempt for mortal men which could on occasion glimmer through the responses given by the Delphic oracle, but it owes most, perhaps, to the privilege accorded by the public to the didactic poet, exhorting and reproving his fellow-men. This same stance was adopted by some early prose writers, and not only in philosophy; Hecataeus, for example (cf. p. 91), declared in his opening sentence that 'the accounts generally given by the Greeks' were 'a lot of rubbish', which he proposed to correct. The style of some of the early philosophers was highly condensed and at times enigmatic, as if they wished to give their dicta the same status as such memorable lines of poetry as: 'A host of kings is bad; let one king rule!' (Homer, *Iliad* ii 204), or 'Fools, knowing not how half exceeds the whole!' (Hesiod, *Works and Days* 40). In particular, Heraclitus of Ephesus (*c*.500) gained a reputation for obscurity, as in: 'They do not understand how it agrees at variance with itself; adjustment under tension, as of bow and lyre' (Heraclitus fr.B51).

A comparable desire to create memorable, succinct, self-contained generalizations seems to have animated a contemporary of Socrates, the materialist philosopher Democritus, if we are to judge by the number of passages taken from him into later anthologies. We may, however, gain a better idea of typical philosophical writing in the late fifth century from an extensive fragment of a work by Antiphon the Sophist, who would not, but for this fragment, occupy an important place in the history of literature. A portion of the fragment runs thus:

... bearing true witness amongst one another is regarded as just and no less as useful in human activities. Now, the man who does this is not just, given that it is just to do no harm to another when one is not oneself harmed; moreover the man who gives evidence, even if his evidence is true, must necessarily harm another in some way and at the same time incur the risk of being harmed himself later because of what he said, inasmuch as through the evidence he gave the man against whom he gave it is convicted and loses his property or his life ...

(Antiphon the Sophist fr. B44)

Antiphon's preoccupation with the moral problem of justice and his readiness to turn a conventional moral view upside-down are equally characteristic of the late fifth century, and it is in that area that the contrast between 'Socratic' and 'Presocratic' is sharpest. On the one side lies a fundamentally sceptical and pragmatic approach to morality, which might on occasion give rise to a cynical exploitation of the means by which juries and assemblies could be manipulated, and on the other side, represented by Socrates, lies an attempt to give traditional moral values an absolute status by building a metaphysical system round them.

III

Many men in the richest and most distinguished families of Athens, particularly young men, cultivated the society of Socrates. This association in the end was fatal to him, for it is unlikely that his prosecution and execution in 399 on a charge of 'injuring the city' by religious innovation and 'corruption of the young' would have succeeded had he not been regarded as the 'teacher' of Alcibiades, who as an exile had done Athens great harm, and of Critias, the leading figure among the 'Thirty Tyrants' who ruled Athens for a time after her surrender to Sparta in 404. Among those who admired Socrates and learned from him there were several who portrayed him in written memoirs as a philosophical teacher; and of these, the two whose works have come down to us intact are Xenophon (cf. p. 101) and Plato. Strong reasons for thinking that Xenophon's *Symposium* was written later than Plato's *Symposium* and in various superficial ways modelled upon it raise the possibility that credit for the invention of a literary genre commemorating the teaching of Socrates might belong to Plato alone, Xenophon and others following where Plato had shown the way. This has the further implication that Plato and Xenophon should not always and necessarily be treated as independent witnesses on matters concerning the personality and beliefs of Socrates himself; where Xenophon is not pursuing his special interest in the management of households and estates, but attempting to illustrate Socratic methods in philosophical argument, he may be drawing upon Plato rather than upon his own recollection of the real Socrates.

In the opening chapter of his four books of Socratic recollections (*Memorabilia*) he makes clear his own intention to demonstrate that Socrates adhered to traditional religious belief and observances, practised and inculcated in others the traditional virtues, decried useless intellectual curiosity, helped his friends — as much by moralistic sermons as by philosophical exposition — to cope with life's problems, and would have kept Alcibiades and Critias on the path of political virtue had they not chosen to close their ears to his wisdom. Anecdotes embodying the witticisms, paradoxes, and warnings uttered by wise and famous men were at all times an important phenomenon of Greek culture; some sarcastic verses of Xenophanes on Pythagoras seem to be an early parody of the genre. Much of the material comprised in Xenophon's *Memorabilia* has this anecdotal character, successive items being introduced by, for example, 'Hermogenes told me . . .', 'Talking once to Clito the sculptor . . .', 'When someone complained . . .', 'Seeing that his young friend Epigenes was in poor physical condition . . .'. Even the more sustained philosophical arguments are firmly set in a narrative context designed to defend Socrates' conventional moral virtues. On topics which Xenophon treats summarily (wisdom, goodness, beauty, and courage), remarking 'it would be a long task to go through all his definitions', Plato has much of infinitely greater weight to say.

Plato was one of the young aristocrats who admired Socrates. Born in 427 — thus twenty-three when Athens surrendered and twenty-eight when Socrates was executed — he suffered profound political disillusionment, first at the murderous and cynical character of the oligarchy of 404, which included some of his own friends and relations, and then at the fate of Socrates a few years after the democratic restoration. Possessed by a passion for philosophy and alienated from the political activities of his own city, he was preoccupied throughout his life by the theoretical possibility of creating a totally stable and enduring political community upon a moral system as invulnerable to rational criticism as a sequence of mathematical theorems. Perhaps influenced by Archytas of Tarentum, who achieved equal distinction in mathematics and in the command of armies, Plato became deeply involved in the dynastic politics of Syracuse, where he was persuaded by Dion, son-in-law of the tyrant Dionysius I, to try to turn the young son of Dionysius into a future 'philosopher-king'. This ambitious project was in the end frustrated by political realities. Plato achieved a more enduring success in a quite different field when he created what came to be known as his 'Academy', a group of colleagues and pupils devoted to continuous study of mathematics and philosophy, meeting in a place called *Akademeia* about a kilometre north-west of Athens. Well before the end of the fifth century teachers of oratory had taken as pupils young men whose ambitions lay in politics and the lawcourts; Plato's Academy, an 'institute' rather than a 'university', differed in that its studies were precisely what we would nowadays call 'academic', and the relations between the participants were probably more collaborative than didactic. The mathematician Eudoxus came to join the Academy; so did the young Aristotle, destined to have vast influence on the future development of philosophy.

Neither Aristotle nor his contemporaries, nor the philosophers of the following century, were Platonists in the sense that they considered it their business to propagate and defend the doctrines of Plato. Indeed, they went on from where Plato left off, and in the process sometimes refined and often overturned axioms and deductions which he regarded as fundamental to his own philosophy. But readers of philosophical literature have read Plato with enthusiasm and awe from the fourth century B.C. onwards; no philosophical writer has had an influence comparable with his, for he possessed, in addition to his intellectual talent, an artistic imagination, sensitivity, and technical skill which made it hard for him, by contrast with academic philosophers in general, ever to write a dull or clumsy sentence. His two monumental works are the *Republic,* an enquiry into 'justice' (the Greek word has connotations of 'honesty', 'uprightness', and 'righteousness'), written in his middle age, and the *Laws,* his last work, an attempt to construct an entire legal code which would make a community virtuous and harmonious, secure and stable. In other works, substantial but not on the same scale as the *Republic* and the *Laws,* he tackles such questions as 'Is the soul immortal?' (*Phaedo,* portraying Socrates' last hours before his execution), 'What is it to "be in love", and of what constituent in the order of things is this experience a particular case?' (*Symposium*), or 'Can one be taught to be good?' (*Meno*). A third category is slight in scale and deliberately restricted in scope, but penetrating and provocative, such as *Ion,* on poetic inspiration, *Lysis,* on affection, and *Laches,* on courage. External information on the times at which Plato's various works were written is deficient, save for the tradition that *Laws* was left unrevised when he died. Anachronistic references to historical events indicate that *Symposium* is later than 385 and *Menexenus* later than 386, while the sequence *Theaetetus–Sophist –Statesman* is assured by references back in the second and third items of the sequence. But in the main the ordering of Plato's works depends on observation of the increase and decrease of linguistic phenomena (such as a particular formula of assent or a particular way of saying 'but . . .') and the increasing prominence, as we approach the *Laws,* of certain rhythms at sentence-end, coupled with avoidance of juxtaposing a vowel or diphthong at word-end with a word which has an initial vowel. Tests of this kind make it possible to group the whole corpus into early, middle, and late strata.

Such a grouping would pose more problems than it solved if it did not square with any intelligible reconstruction of Plato's intellectual development. Fortunately, although substantially differing reconstructions can be offered, and were in fact offered before the potentialities of linguistic and stylistic tests were realized, the reconstruction indicated by the tests is an acceptable one. It is especially so when we acknowledge the likelihood that Plato sometimes discarded earlier hypotheses and adopted new approaches, and when we observe the fact that although in certain works he ranges over a surprising variety of topics (notably in *Phaedrus*) he does not, in any one work, explore implications or recapitulate deductions which are not relevant to the essential enquiry undertaken in that work. What Plato wrote during a period of fifty years must not be treated as if it were a 'Problems of Philosophy' issuing from a press in ten volumes, and with the exception of *Laws, Timaeus,* and certain portions of *Republic,* no one work could be mistaken for a systematic treatise. Plato composed dialogues, dramatic scenes in which people discuss philosophical problems, often enlivened by humour and sometimes touched with intellectual playfulness. Sometimes the scene is strictly dramatic in form, sometimes it is dressed as narrative (with a great deal of 'he said'), and sometimes the introduction has one form and the main text another. Usually (*Meno* is a striking exception) the philosophical topic with which the dialogue will be concerned is not revealed immediately. Two characteristic openings are:

I got back from military service at Potidaea yesterday evening; and as you would expect, arriving after so long away, I was very glad to go to where I usually spend my time. So I went to the wrestling-school of Taureas, the one opposite the sanctuary of Basile, and there I found a lot of people, some of whom I didn't know, but mostly friends of mine. When they saw me coming in unexpectedly, they greeted me, some from here, some from there. And Chaerephon, impulsive as ever, jumped up and left the people he was among and ran towards me. He grasped me by the hand and said, 'Socrates! You've come home safe from the battle! How are you?' There had been a battle at Potidaea not long before I left, and the people here had just heard about it. So I answered him, 'Like this, as you see!'

(Plato, *Charmides* 153AB)

FRIEND Where have you come from, Socrates? Pretty obviously from chasing after that lovely Alcibiades, eh? I saw him the other day, and I thought he was still a very good-looking man — but a *man,* Socrates, between ourselves, with a beard that's getting thicker by now.

SOCRATES Well, what about it? Aren't you an admirer of Homer? And he said that the most attractive age is when the beard starts to grow, the age that Alcibiades is now.

(Plato, *Protagoras* 309A)

The 'I' of the passage from *Charmides* is Socrates, and in *Protagoras* the introductory dramatic scene soon gives place to Socrates' first-person narrative, in response to his friend's entreaty, of his encounter, earlier that day, with Protagoras. The *Republic*, too, is presented as a giant dialogue narrated by Socrates. In all that Plato wrote before the last period of his life Socrates is a major participant, and could fairly be called the 'hero' of each dialogue in the sense that it is he who makes the most powerful destructive criticisms and the most fertile constructive suggestions. One exception to this general rule is *Parmenides,* in which Socrates is still young, unable in the first part of the work to meet criticisms brought by Parmenides against his metaphysical theory, which is laid aside in the dense and subtle argument of the second part. In the late works *Timaeus, Sophist,* and *Statesman* Socrates appears only in the opening section; in *Timaeus* the main burden of what is essentially a continuous exposition is borne by the man after whom the work is named, and in the two latter works the course of the argument is governed by an unnamed philosopher from Elea in south Italy. Finally, in the *Laws* Socrates is not mentioned at all; the entire dialogue is sustained by Clinias (a Cretan), Megillus (a Spartan), and an unnamed Athenian who quickly establishes himself as dominant. If we were wholly deprived of other evidence, we should no doubt adopt the initial working hypothesis that Plato's portrayal of Socrates and others is truthful, so that distinctively Platonic philosophy is to be sought only in the *Laws*. Such a hypothesis, however, is not reconcilable with the 'dramatic dates' of some of the dialogues, which make it extremely hard to reconstruct a consistent development of Socrates' thought. It is still less so with what we are told by Aristotle: that whereas Socrates was concerned with definitions, it was Plato who first postulated the eternal existence of (for example) 'beauty' or 'the beautiful', in which the people and things we call 'beautiful' have only a brief and imperfect participation. Since this Platonic idealism is fundamental to the assumptions and expositions of most Socratic dialogues, it seems that Plato misrepresented his teacher systematically. Had his primary purpose been to furnish material to historians of philosophy and biographers of Socrates, this misrepresentation would merit our contempt. If, however, his readers conceded him the right simultaneously to propagate his own philosophical views and to perpetuate the memory of a great man by putting into his mouth views possibly implied, though never spelled out, in what that man actually said, the case is altered. It must be admitted that we do not know what readers interested in philosophical literature conceded, for although the Socratic dialogue derived some of its features from drama and mime, some from historical tradition, and some from anecdotes attached to the names of wise men, it was essentially a literary innovation of the first order.

Plato's Socrates is diffident, amiable, patient, and urbane, invested with what the Greeks called *eironeia* — not 'irony' in our sense of the word, but a disposition on the part of the knowledge-able and accomplished to affect ignorance and incompetence. In the *Apology,* Plato's literary presentation of the speech made by Socrates when on trial for 'injuring the city' by offending its gods and 'corrupting the young', Socrates relates how the Delphic oracle had said that no one was wiser than he; he interprets this oracular response as meaning that human wisdom is virtually worthless and that his own peculiar wisdom lies in his recognition of that fact (*Apology* 20E–23B). He does not claim to reveal the truth to others, but to elicit it from them by a process of questioning and criticism; in a famous passage of *Theaetetus* (148E–151B) he compares himself to a midwife at the service of those who are 'pregnant in intellect', and warns that associates who desert his company may miscarry or even lose by bad nurture the offspring already brought to birth. Plato on several occasions contrasts the Socratic method with the preferred method of other intellectuals of the period (for example, Pro-tagoras, Prodicus, and Gorgias), who deliver lectures, for a good fee, to admiring audiences.

At a first reading it is easy to accept this contrast as valid; at a second reading, however, we may realize that the appearance of co-operation in the discovery of truth by mutual criticism and the testing of hypotheses is largely an illusion imposed by the veneer of dialogue and by the attractive social graces with which Plato has invested Socrates. Particularly in the second half of a dialogue, Socrates' interlocutor may contribute nothing but simple questions and expressions of assent, and in the *Laws* the intervals between 'How do you mean?' and 'Yes, that's true!' are sometimes so great as to constitute no more than a spare and perfunctory punctuation of what is essentially a continuous exposition by the anonymous Athenian. The depth of the veneer can be gauged accurately in a passage of the *Symposium,* where the guests at a party (the tragic poet Agathon is the host) take turns in making a speech in honour of Eros, the divine personification of sexual love. When it is Socrates' turn, professing to be quite unable to compete with the speech which Agathon has just given, he obtains permission to interrogate Agathon. It does not take him long to extract from Agathon, by dexterous questioning, an admission which demolishes the central theme of the speech, and Agathon concedes defeat.

'Socrates', he said, 'I can't refute you. Let it be as you say.'
'Why, my dear friend, Agathon', said Socrates, 'it's the *truth* that you can't refute. There's nothing difficult in refuting *Socrates*.'

(Plato, *Symposium* 201C)

Socrates then goes on to relate the teaching he received from a certain Arcadian priestess, Diotima by name (whether she is real or fictitious, we do not know). 'I put to her pretty much the same arguments as Agathon put forward to me just now . . . Then she subjected me to the criticisms to which I subjected him . . .' (ibid. 201E) By this device Socrates half-extricates himself from the predicament of a guest who lays down the law, from a position of superior insight, to his host and fellow guests; but only half, for he has plainly charged them all with preferring specious adornment to truth. By narrating a dialogue between himself and Diotima he contributes a little to maintenance of the principle of co-operation in philosophical argument; but only a little, for he explicitly represents Diotima as a 'teacher' and himself as an obsequious pupil who is being 'initiated into mysteries'. Indeed, the last five pages of his story are an increasingly fervent and exalted exhortation by Diotima to struggle free from preoccupation with the beauty of individual people and things and progress through rigorous philosophical discussion to the ineffable bliss of perceiving with the inward eye alone 'Beauty itself, pure, undefiled, uncontaminated'.

The language of the visionary, crashing upon us with the majesty, beauty, and extravagant variety of breakers on a rocky shore, may take us by surprise if we have accepted at its face-value Plato's portrayal of Socrates as a man willing to subject all assumptions and attitudes to fearless objective scrutiny and to be 'carried by the wind of the argument' (*Republic* 394D) to unpredictable destinations. In fact, Plato (and therefore his Socrates) was a man of intense religious faith, whose concern was to find an irrefutable rational basis for believing what he craved to believe: that eternal, immutable Good, which we must necessarily love and desire with a passion beyond all passions when intellectual effort and endurance have persuaded us of its existence, is the ultimate reason for all things. He nowhere proves his theory of eternal 'ideas' or 'forms', for the fact that the evidence of the senses is provisional and corrigible is not even a step on the way unless we add to it the axiom, 'There *must* be *some* way of attaining *certainty* about the universe'. The operation of the further axiom that if we do attain irrefutable knowledge we shall respond to what we know as we respond to good is clearly seen at work in a passage of *Phaedo*, where Socrates speaks of his attempt to come to terms with the scientific speculation of his predecessors:

I once heard someone reading from a book which he said was by Anaxagoras, explaining how it is Intelligence which orders all things and is the reason for them. That reason pleased me, and I thought it was somehow right that Intelligence should be the reason for everything . . . I was glad to think that I had found someone of my own way of thinking — Anaxagoras, that is — to teach me about existing things and tell me the reason for them. I thought he would tell me first whether the earth is flat or round and then, when he had told me that, expound the reason and necessity for it in terms of what is *better*, explaining why it is *better* that the earth should be what it is.

(Plato, *Phaedo* 97B–E)

The possibilities and limitations of rational argument about problems of morality are nowhere more vividly apparent than in the *Republic*, where Socrates' interlocutors, Adimantus and Glaucon, beg him to demonstrate that it is better for a man to be righteous than to be unrighteous 'whether or not he escapes the notice of gods and men', that is, irrespective of any possible reward or penalty. We are all aware of good arguments to the effect that the righteous man is more likely to be happy; equally, we are aware of the impossibility of demonstrating that no unrighteous man ever dies happy in the recollection of a lifetime of successful oppression. But generalization about what is merely likely or unlikely is alien to Plato, who achieves a superficial effect of demonstration by making the participants in the dialogue acquiesce in definitions, analogies, and political and psychological theories which demand closer scrutiny. And the *Republic* ends with a vivid story about the afterlife, using a doctrine of reincarnation and a scheme of reward and punishment irreconcilable with the hypothesis that our lives can ever 'escape the notice of the gods'. Stories of similar character constitute the climax of the argument in *Phaedo* and *Gorgias*. Plato's Socrates admits that their truth is not demonstrable, and he does not claim for them (as men like Parmenides and Empedocles would have claimed) the status of revelation; on the contrary, he insists that he believes them because of their moral value, and it may well be that the choice freely made by an outstandingly good man, articulated with passion, has a more lasting effect on the reader's emotions than the pretentions of a seer or the subtleties of a cool metaphysician.

Plato's faith in the reality of eternal 'ideas', to be apprehended by intellectual effort, did not dispose him favourably to the compromises and dishonesties of practical politics under any existing form of government or to the exercise of the ordinary freedoms which most people seek. The *Republic* is largely devoted to constructing the governmental and educational principles of an ideal state, in which a class system, the philosophically-educated 'guardians' being the ruling class, is an essential element. The notion, however, that Plato was concerned to provide an intellectual basis for the defence of wealth and hereditary privilege against the inroads of democracy is not easily reconciled with the fact that he denies his 'guardians' private property, luxury imports, family ties, and the enjoyment of most forms of art and literature. The oppressive totalitarian character of Plato's ideal community, in *Republic* and *Laws* alike, is, of course, part of his answer to a question which necessarily preoccupied political philosophy in his time: in a world in which weak communities are sometimes obliterated by predatory neighbours and even the strongest communities may be torn apart by recurrent civil war, what political structure, what legislation, will give a community the best chance of survival?

IV

Plato's successor as head of the Academy was Speusippus, but the man who went on from a long apprenticeship in the Academy to develop an original and independent philosophical system of the most lasting importance was Aristotle. Aristotle, son of a doctor and a native of Stagira, in the northern Aegean, spent nearly twenty years at Athens with Plato; on Plato's death he took over an offshoot of the Academy in Asia Minor, went to the Macedonian court as tutor to the young Alexander, returned to Athens some time in the 330s, founded a philosophical school there (the 'Lyceum', a favourite haunt of Socrates a century earlier), and died at Chalcis in 322. His surviving works cover a great range of subjects, including logic, physics, biology, ethics, and literature, and they deserve as much prominence in the history of the sciences as in the history of philosophy. His avid interest in observable phenomena and his desire to explain them by systems of physical and biological laws might be thought of as a reversion to the traditions of early Greek scientific speculation as it was before Socrates, Plato and other Socratics focused attention on moral philosophy and the metaphysics underlying the responses which we express in words such as 'good', 'just' or 'beautiful'. Unlike the early Greeks, however, Aristotle exploited the potentiality of the philosophical 'school' or 'institute', as he knew it, for collective research, notably in using for the construction of his political theory the data assembled by his collaborators from the individual histories of more than a hundred and fifty Greek cities.

The question, 'What is literature?' has already been raised in this chapter; and if we raise it again, as we must, in connection with Aristotle, the candid answer is that his works, exciting though they are to anyone who values contact with genius, cares about the history of human thought, or is willing to learn (from the *Ethics, Poetics,* and *Rhetoric*) some provocative things about himself, are not literature. Aristotle did indeed put into circulation some works which belonged in the genre of philosophical literature, and in composing them he no doubt had regard for the artistic standard expected by an educated reading public; but these we do not possess. The surviving works have the character of textbooks in which elegance, even clarity, is sacrificed to concentration and economy of expression.

Among them two, the *Rhetoric* and the *Poetics,* are of special interest to students of Greek literature. The former, composed at a time when oratory was not only of the highest importance in the internal politics of Athens but also highly regarded as an art-form, examines the techniques of persuading a jury or assembly, and its rules are founded on sensitive observation of what actually works. The *Poetics* similarly must be read not as a prescription for tragic drama in an ideal society but as an analysis of what actually achieves theatrical effect and makes a lasting impression on a discerning and receptive audience. Plato had been hostile to drama, regarding it as setting up bad models for imitation; Aristotle, accepting poetry in general and drama in particular as an essential ingredient of the life of the city-state, addresses himself to the questions, 'What distinctive function does drama perform?' and 'By what means does it most effectively perform that function?'

The encyclopaedic tradition of the Lyceum was continued by Aristotle's pupils, so that the last quarter of the fourth century was phenomenally productive of monographs on scientific, historical, and literary topics. Hardly any of this is known to us except from fragments and citations. Theophrastus is the only author of the group represented by some complete works, among which his *Characters* is unique, even bizarre: a set of thirty highly concentrated sketches of contemptible or disagreeable traits of character, for example, flattery:

. . . and when the other is speaking, he tells everyone else to be quiet, and praises him in his hearing; and whenever he pauses, puts in 'Yes, indeed!', and when he's made a poor joke, laughs at it and stuffs his cloak in his mouth as if unable to restrain his laughter . . . And when the other is going to visit a friend, he runs ahead and says 'He's on his way to you', and then doubles back and says, 'I've told him you're coming'.

(Theophrastus, *Characters* 2.4, 8)

This is not ethics, but rather a vivid realization of the social observation which is one ingredient in Aristotle's analysis (in the *Nicomachean Ethics*) of opposing moral dispositions. The author's intention is not at all clear, and the extant preface does not help our understanding, since it was composed long after Theophrastus' time. But whatever the intention, the result is close to comedy in spirit, and in particular to the portrayal of character which distinguishes the comedy of the late fourth and early third centuries.

8 Classical oratory

Of all the genres of Greek literature, oratory is the least appreciated in our own time; many of us who have read a great deal of Greek epic, drama, history, and philosophy have yet to read a Greek speech. Yet we cannot expect to understand the Greeks' view of their own literature and culture unless we come to terms with their respect for the good orator. Some societies in which the art of writing is unknown develop a very sensitive ear for the spoken word, enjoying the inventiveness, ingenuity, colourful imagery, pathos, and histrionic skill of a man pleading for justice or exhorting an assembly, and there is little doubt that the Greeks of the archaic period were such a society. Homer portrays some Trojan elders (*Iliad* iii 204ff.) as recalling how the Greek envoys who had come to demand the return of Helen differed in stance, gesture, voice, and fluency, and it is noteworthy that they say nothing of the validity of the arguments used; it is the art of the speech as a performance that they remember.

Throughout the history of the Greek city-state decisions which affected the fate of the whole community were taken not by a committee after the digestion of written reports but by an assembly under the immediate impact of speeches. The historians show themselves well aware of this fact in the amount of space which they devote to the presentation of direct speech, and Thucydides (i 22.1f.) treats the discovery of 'what was said' and of 'what was done' as being equally important. Though the outcome of a debate was less predictable in a democratic assembly than in a small oligarchy, deliberative bodies in oligarchies might still be large by modern standards, and political alignments within such a body might be governed by unstable alliances between individuals and groups rather than by the predetermined policies of tightly organized parties. The Athenian democracy, moreover, assigned the task of deciding private lawsuits and criminal prosecutions to large juries (sometimes as many as 501), which, unlike a modern jury, received no technical guidance on points of law. The concept of relevant evidence was acknowledged, but irrelevance was not easily controlled, the techniques available for the investigation of crime were rudimentary, and cross-examination was not employed. Skill in manipulating the thoughts and feelings of a crowd was required by politicians, but not only by them; a man could lose his fortune, his citizen status, even his life, if a jury found him less persuasive than his adversary in court. Litigants could be supported by the speeches of more articulate friends, and they could also seek the advice of men who had devoted much time and thought to the art of pleading, but they had to speak themselves, and they usually made a better impression if they carried the main burden. Since prosecution for offences which would incur punishment by the state was undertaken not by the state itself but by individuals acting out of political zeal or personal enmity, and political, administrative, and military malpractice (or even misjudgement) could be severely punished, the career of a man seeking high standing in the community might well entail both speaking on questions of policy in the assembly and fighting actions in the courts on the widest variety of civil and criminal issues. In court, in order to establish himself in the jury's eyes as trustworthy, he needed to boast of his political career, while his adversary tried to present it in the opposite light, and in the assembly the respect with which he was heard depended on how he had fared in the courts. It could therefore become necessary for the same man to apply himself to 'forensic' and to 'political' oratory, but it was naturally open to the skilled consultant without political ambitions of his own to specialize.

A speaker would have made a deplorable impression if he had read his speech from a written text, and even if he used notes he would suffer by comparison with an adversary who did not; in law and politics, as in war, no standard is satisfactory save that which ensures victory. A speaker therefore had to give a great deal of thought in advance to what he was going to say, and if he was the defendant in a court case he knew that he would have to improvise a rebuttal of unforeseen allegations of bad character and misconduct which might have only marginal relevance to the point at issue. What we read in a Greek speech is not a transcript of the words uttered in court, and its relationship to the speech prepared in advance is hard to determine. There are some reasons to believe that before the written version of a speech was put into circulation it was revised to take account of matter which the composer had not foreseen and to omit matter which had gone down badly. The written speech therefore assumed the character of a political pamphlet, a weapon wielded in the prosecution of a feud, and it endeavours to make us not only respect the composer as a citizen but also fear him as an adversary and admire him as a man of intellectual acumen and artistic sensibility. Few modern readers accord the orator the admiration which he sought. We tend to mistrust technical skill in the service of persuasion; so, indeed, did the Greeks — such mistrust is often expressed in their literature — but the need to win made it indispensable, and the Greeks differed very significantly from us in the sensitivity of their response to the choice, arrangement, and delivery of words. This sensitivity has been dulled to the point of extinction in our own culture by the quick production and consumption of the printed word in immense quantities, the development of pictorial communication, and the importance now assumed by studies and activities which find their most efficient expression in figures and diagrams. Awareness of this difference between our culture and the Greeks' helps us to understand why the functions of oratory were not limited to political deliberation and litigation; great occasions such as international festivals or the burial of the war-dead could be enhanced, on a much greater scale than is acceptable nowadays, by what the Greeks called 'epideictic' oratory, the oratory of display, in which the speaker's concern was to articulate and fortify the sentiments of his audience. Arguments on any topic, designed to stimulate thought by their novelty, were often cast in the form of a speech (the modern equivalent would be an article or essay, perhaps a pamphlet), and by being read aloud at private gatherings they were disseminated far beyond the possessors of the written texts. Compositions of this kind included 'prosecutions' and 'defences' of legendary characters or of persons involved in hypothetical cases, as well as the 'praise' or 'blame' of creatures, inventions, commodities or abstractions; in Plato's

Symposium the guests take it in turn to extemporize speeches in praise of Eros, the deity who personifies the experiences of falling in love and being in love.

It was undoubtedly the importance of the spoken word in politics and law — that is to say, in the life of the community — which diverted so much intellectual energy in the second half of the fifth century B.C. into the analysis and systematization of the techniques of persuasion, and away from scientific activity. The 'sophists', who in their way performed the function now performed for a very much larger section of society by tertiary education, interested themselves in a great range of subjects, from physics and biology to logic and ethics (cf. p. 106), but their pupils were commonly motivated by an ambition to attain high standing in the community, through skill in persuasive speaking. In Aristophanes' *Clouds*, where Socrates is caricatured as a sophist, the old man who tries to learn from him wants above all to know how to defeat his creditors in court, for Socrates knows how to 'make wrong appear right'. However great the misunderstanding of Socrates' interests and priorities, the comic poet's notion of sophistic teaching is not wholly mistaken; a chain of affinities links the practical techniques of persuasive speech with intellectual exercises in 'praising and blaming the same thing' (an educational practice ascribed to the sophist Protagoras) and philosophical enquiry into the fragility of inference from the evidence of one's senses.

II

It seems to have been between 430 and 420 B.C. that the practice of circulating speeches in writing began at Athens; it may possibly have begun a little earlier in Sicily. Tradition, founded in the first place on experience and memory and thereafter sustained by reference to the available allusions and representations in comedy and history, regarded Pericles as the supreme political orator. He died in 429, and no Periclean speech was transmitted in written form; the relation between what he actually said on certain occasions and the highly condensed, sophisticated speeches put into his mouth by Thucydides is controversial (cf. p. 98). The earliest orator whose speeches could be read by posterity was Antiphon, active in Athenian anti-democratic circles as a political consultant but unobtrusive in public life until he took part in the revolution of 411 and was executed for treason in the following year. What we have of his work all concerns homicide, and it includes three quartets of speeches on imaginary cases — two by the prosecution, and two for the defence, in each case. These oratorical exercises may not be by Antiphon himself, but there is no reason to dismiss them as late forgeries, and some reason to think that they may be a little earlier than Antiphon; theoretical works on oratory, accompanied by the construction of models and exercises, may perhaps antedate the publication of written versions of speeches composed for actual occasions. It is also necessary to remember that Athenian booksellers in the fourth century B.C. liked to ascribe to one or another of a small number of famous orators many speeches actually composed by little-known individuals, very much as London music-publishers in the late eighteenth century sold under the name of Haydn a great deal of music which was not his. The Greeks themselves took it for granted, and did not think it pedantic or over-ingenious to suspect, that a speech which bore the name of X might not be by X. These uncertainties frustrate attempts to write the biography of an individual orator or to characterize his personal range of styles, but they do not prevent us from studying the history of oratory as a genre, for the speeches sold under the name of X in the fourth century and catalogued as his in the Alexandrian Library a century later were normally the products of his period and ambience.

The language of oratory in the late fifth century seems to have been exuberant and inventive. Antiphon, like Thucydides, had a penchant for rare words, and perhaps coined some (though before speaking with assurance of the coining of words we would need much more evidence than we have). Gorgias, a Sicilian teacher of oratory well known at Athens, interested more in artistic and intellectual display than in the practicalities of law and politics, exploited to an exaggerated degree the potential of the Greek language for assonance and symmetry, as, for example, in his *Praise of Helen* (he calls it a *paignion*, 'conceit' or 'entertainment'), where he argues that Helen of Troy is not to be blamed for going off with Paris.

It was either by the wishes (*boulēmata*) of Fortune and the counsels (*bouleumata*) of the gods and the decrees (*psēphismata*) of Necessity that she did what she did, or carried off by force, or persuaded by argument, or seized by Love. In the first case, her accuser merits accusation; for it is impossible by human forethought (*promēthiā*) to thwart the determination (*prothūmiā*) of a god. For it is the law of nature not that the stronger should be thwarted by the weaker, but that the weaker should be ruled (*arkhesthai*) and led (*agesthai*) by the stronger.

(Gorgias, *Helen* 6)

Gorgias's style had enduring influence, though in forms much more refined and subtle than the example displays, on epideictic oratory, which from the beginning of the fourth century was clearly differentiated in style from forensic and political oratory. At the same time a sharper demarcation between prose and poetry established itself rapidly. There are still poetic constructions and expressions in the long speech *On the Mysteries* composed in his own defence by the politician Andocides in 400/399, but by that time a style in touch with the spoken language, but invested with a force and dignity lacking in everyday speech, was already establishing itself as the appropriate medium for the courts and the assembly.

III

Among the orators whose reputations have best stood the test of time is Lysias, the son of a wealthy Syracusan arms-manufacturer long resident at Athens; as an alien, he was debarred from exercising the rights of an Athenian citizen, but after the 'Thirty Tyrants', imposed on Athens by the enemy at the end of the Peloponnesian War, had killed his brother, he joined the democratic forces in exile and was able to contribute to their restoration through his business connections. His work for a variety of litigants displays an ability to match the style and argument of a speech to individual personalities, as the following three examples show. The first speaker is a husband who has trapped and killed his wife's lover; the second, a cripple whose right to a state subsidy has been questioned; and the third, a man whose qualification to serve on the Council is in dispute.

So off went the old woman, and straight away I was in a great turmoil, and everything came into my mind, and I was full of suspicion, when I thought how I'd been locked in the bedroom and I remembered how that night the courtyard door creaked, and the outer door too, which had never happened before, and I got the impression that my wife had had make-up on. All this came into my mind, and I was full of suspicion.

(Lysias, *On the Murder of Eratosthenes* 17)

About my riding horses — to which he had the audacity to refer, with no fear of Fortune and no shame in front of you — there's not much I need say. It seems to me that all those who labour under a misfortune use their wits above all in looking for some way to cope with the suffering inflicted on them, some way that will most save them distress. I'm one of them, and, given the plight I'm in, riding is the most comfortable way I've found of going on any journey that's more than the minimum.

(Lysias, *Defence of the Cripple* 10)

Now, first, you must realize that no man is by nature either oligarchic or democratic; whatever constitution is to the advantage of an individual, that is the one which he wants to see established . . . It is not, therefore, difficult to see that the subject of conflicts is not the constitution, but the personal advantage of the individual. So you should assess the loyalty of citizens by looking at their political conduct under the democracy and asking whether they stood to gain anything by revolution.

(Lysias, *Defence on a charge of anti-democratic activity* 8, 10)

One of the surviving speeches of Lysias is the accusation which he himself made against a member of the Thirty Tyrants, Eratosthenes (unconnected with the adulterer in the excerpt above); it is a speech of great lucidity and force, and ends with seven Greek words which require some amplification to pass muster as English, literally, 'I-shall-stop accusing. You-have-heard, you-have-seen, you-have-undergone, you-have. Judge.' That is to say, 'Here I end my speech. You have heard my words. You have seen him. You have suffered under him. You have him. Now judge him!' (Lysias, *Prosecution of Eratosthenes* 100).

IV

From the period 403–390 we possess half a dozen forensic speeches composed by Isocrates, who grew up during the Peloponnesian War and lived to see the decisive victory of Philip over the Greek city-states, dying in 338 at the age of ninety-eight. He was never an active politician, and in middle age he abandoned the practice of writing for litigants; instead, he established a school of oratory. As a teacher of oratory he inevitably incurred much the same odium as the sophists of the previous generation, being vulnerable to the allegation that in return for payment he taught people who were in the wrong how to persuade a jury that they were in the right. His teaching, however, had little bearing on the practice of the lawcourts; it assumed and gave expression to generally acceptable moral values, aligned itself with conservative sentiment on political and economic issues, and adopted a notion of the Athenian past which was patriotic, moralistic, and altogether lacking in the precision and discrimination demanded by genuine historical curiosity. During the second half of his life he published a number of essays, cast in the form of speeches, on major political issues. They preach the need for a reform of attitudes but avoid detailed discussion of the relation between ends and means in political and administrative procedures. Like Xenophon and no doubt many others who looked at the mid-fourth century with eyes which had seen the endless shifts of the balance of power between the city-states, he was preoccupied with the problem of Greek disunity, and he saw in Philip of Macedon a potential leader of Greeks and Macedonians in a long and profitable war against the Persian Empire.

At eighty-two Isocrates wrote a work, *On the Exchange* (the title is derived from a certain procedure in the Athenian system of taxation), in which he explains and defends his own concept of culture and his own system of education through oratory. His attitude to serious intellectual activity is strikingly patronizing and philistine. Mathematics and astronomy, for example, he regards as studies which attract the ingenious young and perform a useful function in sharpening their wits, as well as keeping them away from more sensual pastimes, but do not merit the attention of mature men. And the fact that philosophers disagree fundamentally on metaphysical questions seems to him a good reason for wasting no time on metaphysics. When he praises originality, he does not mean the radical originality which exposes the weakness of traditional belief, but inventiveness in the service of traditional virtues. For him, the articulation of argument and exhortation fortifies the character of the speaker as father, citizen, soldier, and Greek and enhances the solidarity and endurance of the family, the city, and the civilized world. He devoted immense care to the architecture of language, and the complexity of a typical Isocratean sentence contrasts with the simple symmetries and assonances of Gorgias. The following example is set out in print in a way designed to display its structure.

I assert
> that to acquire the requisite knowledge of the modes of utterance
>> on which all composition and delivery of discourse is founded
>>> is not among the most difficult of tasks,
>>>> provided that one puts oneself in the hands
>>>>> not of those who make easy promises
>>>>> but of those who have real understanding of the subject,
> but to choose the elements appropriate for any given occasion
>> and to combine them one with another
>> and to order them suitably
>> and moreover to make no misjudgment of the occasion
>>>>>> but to elaborate the thought of the whole speech becomingly
>>>>>> and to attain harmony and art in language
>> requires great preparation
>> and is a task for a vigorous and inventive mind;
and that it is necessary
> that the pupil,
>> in addition to the natural endowment which is indispensable,
>> should learn the different kinds of speech
>> and be practised in their use,
> while the teacher
>> should be able to expound some lessons with such thoroughness
>> as to omit nothing of what can be transmitted in teaching,
>> and for the rest should make himself an example of such a kind
>>> that those who are modelled on him
>>>>> and capable of imitating him
>>> should be recognized unquestionably as speaking
>>>> more artistically and more acceptably than all others.

(Isocrates, *Against the Sophists* 16–18)

V

There is a striking contrast between Isocrates and the greatest of the fourth-century orators, Demosthenes. Demosthenes came into prominence in Athenian politics in the 350s; by that time he had already proved himself a forensic speaker of considerable power and elegance and a tenacious adversary, for he had brought actions against the guardians who had handled his inheritance from his father during his adolescence, and through that he had been caught up in a nexus of long-standing feuds. A set of massive speeches written in the period 355–352 displays his deep involvement with an influential group in political life. These speeches are rarely read in translation nowadays; to disentangle their intricate and allusive arguments requires patience and much technical knowledge. It is easier for the modern reader to appreciate the shorter speeches, the *Philippics* and *Olynthiacs*, charged with passion and scorn, in which Demosthenes sought to encourage Athenian resistance to Philip of Macedon. After Philip's victory in 338, positive attempts to organize opposition to the Macedonians became imprudent and pointless. When Philip's son, Alexander the Great, died in 323, revolt flared up; Demosthenes played a part in this revolt, but it failed, and he killed himself in 322 to avoid arrest and execution. He is commonly admired as a champion of democracy against absolute monarchy and of the small, proud city-state against the military might of an alien conqueror. He was that among other things; but two centuries later Polybius (xviii 14) made the point that Demosthenes was too free in branding as 'traitors' men in many parts of Greece who sided with Philip as a refuge from Spartan aggression and were not unreasonably cool towards the maintenance of Athenian power.

Like Isocrates, Demosthenes took great artistic trouble; they both avoided 'hiatus' (the placing of a word which begins with a vowel immediately after a word ending with a vowel), and Demosthenes introduced a further refinement, avoiding any combination of words which would create a succession of more than two syllables scanned 'short' by the rules of Greek metre. Greek commonly admits of alternative orderings of the words in a clause, and though the principles governing a writer's choice between the alternatives are reasonably well understood, we cannot expect to assess the subtleties with confidence; hence we cannot easily pass judgement on the 'naturalness' of Demosthenes' language. We can, however, observe that whereas the elaborate structuring of Isocrates' prose distracts our attention from the content, Demosthenes often conveys an impression of spontaneity which it is fair to suppose he achieved by spending twice as much time on achieving it as lesser men spent on displaying a more obvious virtuosity of style. In the following passage he introduces a long argument to the effect that a decree proposed by a certain Aristocrates is illegal.

It is only right, I think, that having promised to demonstrate three points — one, that the decree proposed is contrary to law; secondly, that it is disadvantageous to our city; and thirdly, that the beneficiary of the proposal does not merit what he is offered — I should give you, who will hear my argument, the freedom to choose what you wish to hear first, what second, and what last. Consider your preference, so that I may deal with that first. You prefer the argument about illegality? Very well, I will speak about that.

(Demosthenes, *Prosecution of Aristocrates* 18f.)

We do not normally expect to find, in the small fraction of Greek oratory which has survived, two speeches which are concerned with the same case — indeed, we do not as a rule know whether the speech which we read was a successful or unsuccessful plea — but two famous occasions on which Demosthenes found himself in opposition to Aeschines furnish exceptions. In 343 Demosthenes prosecuted Aeschines for betraying Athenian interests on an embassy (in which they both participated) to Philip of Macedon, and his speech *On the Misconduct of the Embassy* may be read in conjunction with Aeschines' defence; and Aeschines' *Prosecution of Ctesiphon,* delivered in 330, is answered by Demosthenes' *On the Crown,* the most famous of Greek speeches, in which Demosthenes presents a justification of his own policies in the years which culminated in Philip's final victory. The speech is massive, but charged throughout with vigour, pathos and drama; a random sample may convey its qualities.

Everyone, everywhere, lets the past go, and no one offers advice about it. It is the future or the present that requires the adviser to perform his function. On that occasion it was apparent that some of our perils lay ahead, while others were already upon us; look at the policy I chose *then,* don't carp at me for the outcome. All things turn out in the end as God wills; it is choice of policy, and that alone, which reveals the mind of the adviser . . . If the hurricane was too strong, not just for us, but for all the Greek world, what can be done? As if a ship-owner, who had done everything for the safety of his ship and equipped it in a way which, to the best of his belief, would bring it through safely, and then met a storm, and the tackle were damaged, or even completely smashed, and someone blamed him for the wreck! 'It wasn't my hand on the tiller', he would say — just as I wasn't a general — 'and I was not the master of Fate; she is the mistress of everything.'

(Demosthenes, On the Crown 192–4)

Nothing illustrates the Greeks' interest in oratory more vividly than the fact that side by side with political speeches on issues of the greatest magnitude, such as *On the Crown,* ancient critics valued and transmitted speeches written for unimportant litigants involved in petty squabbles. Granted that we may err in assessing the importance of a man about whom we may by chance know nothing else, we can at least be sure that the erosion of a field by a neighbour's blocking of a stream was not an event upon which the fortunes of Athens turned; but it is precisely on cases of such a kind that Demosthenes on occasion employed his most sensitive craftsmanship. These 'private' speeches, together with the surviving speeches of an orator, Isaeus, of the generation before Demosthenes (all concerned with disputed wills, though we know that Isaeus handled other types of case too), have a peculiar value in that they illustrate the social attitudes and values of classical Athens in the fourth century B.C., and the best of them bring Athens vividly to life.

9 Greek literature 300–50 B.C.

I

The conquests of Philip, who died in 336 B.C., and Alexander, who died in 323, had an immense impact on the life and literature of Greece. Greek language and culture were spread, more or less thinly, over an area from Marseilles to the frontier of India, and from the Crimea to Egypt. In huge countries like Egypt and Syria Greek communities, surrounded by a sea of alien subjects, hugged their education and their language as marks of their status and as reminders of what they were and what they were resolved to remain. The new city of Alexandria, where the first Ptolemies lavished on the Museum and the Library the fabulous wealth of Egypt, soon became the greatest centre of literature and scholarship; except in philosophy, the ascendancy of Athens became more and more a sentimental memory of past glories. A new cosmopolitanism had become possible: a man could leave the city of his birth and make a career in Egypt, or the distant East. Wherever he went, he would find the same Greek framework of education and culture, gymnasium and theatre; and the philosophical schools, like the mystery cults, were the same everywhere.

In this vast world, which suddenly dwarfed the old city-states, a vast amount of literature was produced. We know the names, for instance, of hundreds of historians, of whose work we possess either fragments or nothing at all; and of 130 tragic poets, of whose complete output there survives a total of 403 lines of poetry — less than a third of one tragedy. In this period every city had its theatre, and tragedies, both new compositions and revivals of the fifth-century classics, were constantly performed. Epics continued to be written, philosophers constructed systems, scholars edited texts and established the study of grammar, technical and scientific work was produced in immense quantities. At a less pretentious level, works of pure entertainment abounded — the first novel falls into this period, as do fantasy travel books, pornographic mimes, memoirs, anecdotes. We shall be discussing the great survivors, whose work is still accessible and still read, but we must remember that their work formed only a tiny fraction of a huge literature. Greek was so much the universal literary language that Babylonians, Egyptians, Jews and Romans began to write in Greek. It was also a period in which we find emancipated women. A number of women poets — Anyte, Erinna, Moero, Nossis — have left extant poems, and there were a few women philosophers, as well as formidable queens.

In the third century there was a great output of poetry, of philosophy, and also of scholarly work on texts, language and grammar; in the second, the dominant forms were history and physical science. In the late second century and early first, except for isolated figures (Posidonius, Parthenius), we are aware of an exhaustion, and originality is hard to find; the ravages of the Greek world by Rome will partly explain this. Most of the great Greek cities were sacked by Roman armies, and some had gone out of existence. Only with the Roman Empire does Greek literature revive.

Two more preliminary remarks. First, Hellenistic literature has survived in an unrepresentative form: we have a lot of poetry, but the literary prose of the period is almost completely lost. Taste in prose style changed with the rise, about 50 B.C., of 'Atticism' — the insistence on following the style of the Athenian writers of the fifth and fourth century — and this change condemned the writings of the last 250 years; felt to be in bad taste, they were left unread. The orators and rhetorical historians are to us little more than names. Second, the technical works which survive are not literary and can be barely mentioned. Greek science and mathematics reached their height at this time. Aristarchus of Samos held that the earth and the planets revolved round the Sun; Archimedes invented hydrostatics and built a planetarium; Euclid wrote textbooks on geometry which satisfied the world for 2000 years; Herophilus discovered the nervous system, and Erasistratus came close to discovering the circulation of the blood; Heron devised, but did not exploit, machines which worked by steam. In the fifth century, Empedocles could produce work which claimed both to be scientific and also to be literature, but by now progress and specialization meant that scientific writings were purely technical, with no literary claims or qualities.

After the rise of prose as the natural medium for the expression of serious thought, which took place about 400 B.C., the fourth century marked, for various reasons, a gap, a radical break, in the poetical tradition of Greece. Only New Comedy, whose beauties are those of an art close to prosaic and everyday reality, produced a poet who could be felt to rival Plato or Demosthenes. The 'higher' genres of poetry, those which made great claims and were written in the high style, are little seen: no epic, lyric, or tragic poet of the fourth century was highly regarded either by contemporaries or by posterity. Poetry began to revive about 320 B.C. with the important but enigmatic figure of Philetas of Cos. His work was praised by Theocritus and Callimachus, and also by their Roman admirers, Propertius and Ovid; but we know painfully little of it. He wrote poems with mythological titles (*Demeter, Hermes*), short poems of various content (*Paegnia*, 'Amusements'), love poetry about a lady named Bittis — and books in prose on rare words in earlier poetry. He was both a poet and a scholar, and his scholarly work made him so famous that in the third century there were already jokes about him in Athenian comedy. He lived in Alexandria, where the Ptolemies were amassing an unrivalled collection of books and paid scholars to live, tax-free, attached to the Museum, and he was put in charge of the education of the Crown Prince. The great quality of his poetry was its combination of small scale and artistic refinement, and it was this which made him a symbolic figure for later poets with the same ideal. He is typical of them, too, in combining poetry and scholarship. This did not simply mean that poets, in order to make a living, had to have university positions, a situation we know today, but that the scholarly researches of men like Philetas, Callimachus, Apollonius, and Euphorion formed a vital part of their poetry. They came upon material which fascinated them — recherché myths, local histories, geographical details, rare poetical usages — which they then polished and displayed in their own poems.

We can form a real view of Callimachus (writing *c.*280–240 B.C.). He, too, was a scholar as well as a poet, author of prose works on such subjects as *Rivers of the World, Names of the Months in Different Nations and Cities,* and above all a *Catalogue of All Greek Literature (Pinakes),* on a monumental scale — 120 books — in which the entire body of Greek literature was divided into classes (epic, philosophy, tragedy, etc.), and the names of all the writers were listed in alphabetical order, with a short account of the life of each and a list of his works. This great work, which was the basis of all later Greek literary histories, made orderly and accessible the huge mass of books brought together by the Ptolemies in the Library.

In poetry, his most important work, the *Aitia* ('Origins') survives only in fragments, as does his short epic, the *Hecale,* and his *Iambic Poems.* Six *Hymns* have survived intact, and sixty short epigrams; and we know a great deal about some of the works which are not now complete, as some of the fragments are very long. The *Aitia* dealt with aetiological myths and stories, which explain customs or titles or works of art of his own day. The style is dryly humorous, very learned and allusive, unsentimental, and aims always to surprise the reader. If there is a gap of one word in his text, it is hardly ever possible to be sure what it was. One of its most famous episodes tells of Acontius' love for Cydippe, whom he tricked by putting into her way an apple on which he had written, 'By Artemis, I will marry Acontius'. She unsuspectingly read it aloud, and the goddess Artemis held her to the oath; three attempts to marry her to another man were frustrated by attacks of illness, and at last Apollo told her father to marry her to Acontius:

And then to Artemis they kept her word:
Girls spoke the marriage-song, no more deferred.
Would you have taken, for that night alone,
When you, Acontius, touched her maiden zone,
Iphiclus' foot that skimmed the ears of wheat,
Or all the gold of Midas' Phrygian seat?
I fancy not; and all would vote with me
Who've felt the cruel god's divinity.
A mighty clan from that old union came;
For still they dwell, Acontiads by name,
Your sons, my Cean friend, on Cean ground,
High honoured. Now this love of yours I found

In Xenomedes' *Cean History*:
He wrote your island story thoroughly . . .
              (Callimachus, fr. 75.42–55)

Callimachus is a translator's despair, but this passage perhaps
illustrates the dry tone (the scholarly poet names his source), the
learning (Iphiclus could run across a field of corn without
bending the ears), and the unexpectedness of the style. The poem
is the model of Ovid's *Fasti* and to some extent of his *Metamorph-
oses*, too.

In the *Hymn to Zeus* Callimachus dealt with the birth of the god.
It was generally believed that Zeus was born in Crete, so he
decides in favour of an obscurer version — that the god was born
in Arcadia ('Cretans are always liars', Callimachus observes
archly, quoting the archaic Cretan Epimenides). At that time, he
goes on, Arcadia was riverless ('Azenis', 'parched land', was an
old name for Arcadia: Callimachus wrote a prose treatise on
Changes of Name of Islands and Cities), and Zeus' mother Rhea could
find no water to wash herself and the new-born baby:

> Not yet flowed mighty Ladon, nor the fall
> Of Erymanthus, whitest stream of all;
> Azenis parching lay, though history
> Would call her soon 'well-watered Arcady':
> Soon, but not yet. When Rhea's travail neared,
> Many the oaks Iaon moist upreared,
> Many the waggons Melas had to bear;
> Above Carïon adders built their lair,
> Where all is water now; the traveller spent
> O'er Crathis and Metope's shingle went,
> And went athirst, that water underfoot . . .
>   (Callimachus, *Hymns* i 18–27)

The author of *Rivers of the World* versifies part of his section on
Arcadia, with careful variation and the straight-faced humour of
treating these obscure little streams as if they were mighty rivers.
Of course, these *Hymns* are the work of a poet for whom the old
myths and the old gods are no longer a matter of belief, nor of
serious concern; they form a marvellous distant world, glamorous
and slightly comical, with which he can amuse himself and his
cultured reader, who picks up the allusions and hints which the

poet sows with so deft and light a hand. In classical Greek poetry myth was the vehicle of serious thought and reflection about the gods and the world; with Callimachus we see the origin of the beautiful but purely decorative myths of Ovid, or Titian, or Handel's *Acis and Galatea,* or Shakespeare's *Venus and Adonis.* Another aspect of Callimachus which proved influential was his love of polemic. He often defends his own verse and hits back at his critics, in a style which is ironical, superior, and full of insulting images; his critics 'bray like donkeys', while he 'sings like the cicada': the big scale of their poetry makes it like the filthy River Euphrates, while his is a pure small fountain. These passages, written from the stand-point of one attacked by numerous adversaries, show that he was by no means a literary dictator in his lifetime. They were much imitated by Virgil, Horace, and Propertius.

II

Contemporary with Callimachus flourished Theocritus of Syracuse (writing *c.*275–260 B.C.). He, too, after failing to find patronage in Sicily (*Idyll* XVI), made his way to Alexandria (XVII, XV); he also was at home on Cos (VII), the island where King Ptolemy II, patron of Callimachus and Theocritus, was born. He is not known to have written anything in prose, but he was a learned poet, who wrote poems in the manner and metre of Alcaeus, in the obsolete Lesbian dialect of 350 years earlier (XXVIII–XXXI) — this artificial *tour de force* anticipates Horace's Latin poems in imitation of Alcaeus and other archaic lyric poets — and also poems in the manner of Homeric Hymns and other remote models. His lasting achievement, however, was the invention of pastoral verse in its classic form. His pastoral poems (I, III, V, VI, VII, XI) are mimes written in hexameter verse, although that description is paradoxical. The hexameter, the metre of Homer, was the grandest of Greek metres and the least like ordinary speech, with overtones of battle and heroism; the mime was a realistic performance, sometimes very crudely so, both in subject and in style. To combine them is a highly sophisticated idea, producing an effect of poignant incongruity.

One might perhaps compare Cocteau making a film of the fairy tale of Beauty and the Beast. Theocritus adds the vital ingredient of a new melodiousness in his verse. He writes these poems in the Doric dialect, which was by tradition not used for hexameters; it was full of long open vowels, especially ā and ō, and Theocritus produces the most beautiful sound patterns. He uses a vocabulary mostly simple, often repeating such adjectives as 'sweet', 'lovely', 'bad', to convey the naïveté of his rustic speakers, but varying it artfully with rare words, coinages of his own, and poetic echoes: *he* is not a simple soul like his shepherds and cowherds. The shepherds sing of love and song; they compete with each other in singing, they describe charming rustic places, and tell of Pan and the Nymphs.

A reader of Milton's *Lycidas* will have some idea of the style of Theocritus at his most learned. Perhaps certain poems of Tennyson might suggest the style at its sweetest — the song in *The Lotos-Eaters* ('There is sweet music here . . .') or that in *The Princess* ('Come down, o maid, from yonder mountain height'). In this passage, the shepherd Thyrsis is singing of the death of Daphnis, who died for love: at the last he addresses the pastoral god Pan:

'O Pan, O Pan, where'er thou rangest now —
Lycaeus' hill-top or tall Maenalus —
Come to the isle of Sicily, and leave
The cairn of Hélicê, and the towering tomb
Where Arcas lies, which even the gods admire.'

Muses, forgo, forgo the pastoral song.

'Master, approach: take to thee this fair pipe
Bedded in wax that breathes of honey still,
Bound at the lip with twine. For Love has come
To hale me off unto the house of Death.'

Muses, forgo, forgo the pastoral song.

'Now let the briar and the thistle flower
With violets; and the fair narcissus bloom
On junipers: let all things go awry,
And pines grow pears, since Daphnis is for death.
Let stags pursue the hounds, and from the hills
The screeching owls outsing the nightingales.'

Muses, forgo, forgo the pastoral song.

So said he then — no more. And Aphrodite
Was fain to raise him; but the Destinies
Had spun his thread right out. So Daphnis went
Down-stream: the whirlpool closed above his head,
The head of him whom all the Muses loved,
Of him from whom the Nymphs were not estranged.
  (Theocritus 1 123–42, translation Sir W. Marris)

Other poems of Theocritus are not strictly pastoral. In II a lovelorn girl tries by magic to win back the lover who has abandoned her. In XV two bourgeois housewives go on an expedition to see a religious festival and hear a hymn; the beauty of the poem lies in the skill with which the ordinary speech of the ladies, their proverbial expressions, their complaints about their husbands, their scolding of the servants, is versified in elegant hexameters, full of contrasts and deft humour. Other poems are short epic narratives (XIII, XXII, XXIV) or rustic mimes of a less pretty and more realistic sort (IV, X). All are skilful and some are charming; Theocritus shows great skill in varying his style to suit all these different forms. But it was the pastorals which, by way of Virgil's *Eclogues,* left an undying mark on European literature. After Theocritus other poets carried on his manner, and some of their poems pass as the work of Theocritus himself ([Theocritus] VIII, IX). Moschus produced a charming, light-hearted *Europa* on the abduction of the young princess by the beautiful bull who is really Zeus; Bion wrote a *Lament for Adonis* which successfully combines with correct Greek form the plangent and exotic Eastern lament.

Both Callimachus and Theocritus avoided the form of the single long poem, putting their emphasis on perfection of technique on a small scale; the *Aitia* is not an exception, as it consists of a series of short poems cleverly strung together. Apollonius of Rhodes, who was Head of the Alexandrian Library about 250 B.C. and was active as a scholar, also produced a long poem, the *Argonautica,* an epic on the voyage of Jason and the Argonauts to fetch the Golden Fleece. There is an ancient tradition that Callimachus quarrelled violently with him over his poem, but this may well be an invention. Apollonius, too, valued technical refinement and sophistication; his poem is far from being a mere attempt to produce another *Odyssey,* and he actually echoes Callimachus' poems in several places. It is hard to believe that they were opponents on principle, although they may indeed have fallen out. The literary men living together in Alexandria were a quarrelsome lot, and three of Callimachus' *Iambic Poems* dealt with disputes among them. The great achievement of Apollonius is his treatment in book iii of the love of Medea for Jason; in the end she brings herself to betray her father and her country for the glamorous hero. She is a young girl falling in love for the first time, but she is also a formidable sorceress: as she goes to meet Jason, the Colchians avoid her gaze, for she may have the Evil Eye. Psychological complexity, of a sort unknown in the Homeric epics, is a great feature of this epic. Jason is beautiful but weak — he is repeatedly shown despairing and helpless — and the essentially unheroic character of the old fairy story (of the lucky prince who is helped in his ordeals by a loving princess) is brought out to the full. He acquiesces in Medea's passion because he needs her help; but the poet gives us clear hints (iii.997, iv.355ff.) of what will happen after the end of the poem — Jason will desert her, and she will murder his new bride and her own children. The portrayal of Medea served as a model for Virgil's portrayal of Dido in *Aeneid* book iv, the greatest and most influential depiction in Latin literature of a woman in love; and even in comparison with Virgil, Apollonius holds his own. In some ways he excels Virgil: the coherence of the heroine's complex character is more convincingly handled, for instance. Medea is a real sorceress, whose powers are vital to the plot; but when Dido turns to magic the effect, though grandiose, is essentially inorganic.

In this passage Medea, who after long mental struggle has resolved to save Jason from her father, has come to meet him for the first time. She brings the magic ointment which will enable him to yoke the fire-breathing bulls and plough the field for the sowing of the dragon's teeth. Jason has made a wheedling speech, asking her to save him as Ariadne saved Theseus; he leads her to believe that Theseus was true to Ariadne, although we know that he in fact deserted her — as Jason will desert Medea.

Hearing his courtesies
Blissfully smiling did she her eyes abash.
By his praise in a confusion of her heart
Raised up, she lifted up her eyes to his,
But found no single word to make a start,
Striving all to express in one packed voicing.
Out of her scented sash
The charm she took, unsparing, and he rejoicing
Received it in his hands: at his desire
She would have plucked the very life from her breast
And given it him, such bright and beautiful fire
On Jason's yellow hair, Love's influence, played.
The flashings of her eyes he captive made,
And all her heart its secret warmth discloses,
Melting like morning dew upon the roses
That warm day melts; and now
Shyly they to the ground their eyes abase,
And now gaze at each other face to face,
Each smiling love under a shining brow.

> (Apollonius, *Argonautica* iii 1008–24, translation G. Allen)

In this passage the speechlessness of the bashful lovers conveys a feeling of the conversation of their souls, existing for the moment outside time.

The poem, despite the poet's attempt at unity, remains essentially episodic. This is in part because of the nature of the story — the Argo sails to Colchis and back again, and the Argonauts have a series of adventures in the different places they pass (and the poet is able to air his theories about geography, taking his characters by some disputed routes) — but also because of Apollonius' own talents and limitations. A number of scenes and tableaux succeed memorably, such as Jason's affair with Hypsipyle on Lemnos (i 610ff.), the forced marriage of Jason and Medea, bedding on the Golden Fleece in a sacred cave (iv 1129ff.), or the exquisitely humorous and delicate scene of the great goddesses Hera and Athena forced to visit Aphrodite to ask for her help (they find her washing her hair, and the dialogue, though in epic form, is pure comedy of manners: iii 1ff.). But Apollonius feels obliged to leave nothing out, and some episodes are all too clearly there only because he recognized an obligation to include them. His skill lies in presenting scenes of melancholy and in beautiful descriptions of effects of light: this, and the civilized attitude of his heroes, who find themselves almost as much at a loss in a world of supernatural perils and rewards as Apollonius and his own contemporaries would have been, may be thought strange equipment for an epic poem, and many of Apollonius' great successes seem in a way to be anti-epic in feeling.

The style of the poem shows his learning. A long series of variants on Homeric phrases and lines, with a sharp eye for every chance to use and implicitly explain any disputed or unique word in the Homeric text, are effects hard indeed to convey in a translation. They also can become fatiguing to a reader, especially as Apollonius does not, of course, follow Homer in the naïve practice of repeating lines and passages unchanged — he and his audience are too sophisticated for that; and so there are no unstressed passages where one can rest from the exacting complexity of the style.

All three of these poets were contemporaries in the one great generation of Alexandrian poetry. Also writing at the same time (*c.*260 B.C.) was the mime-writer Herodas (sometimes called Herondas), eight of whose dramatic scenes (*c.*60–100 lines each) came to light in 1891 on a papyrus roll. In the unusual metre of limping iambics (an iambic line ending not $\cup - \cup -$ but $\cup - - -$), he depicts scenes from real life. A virtuous wife whose husband is abroad is tempted by an old procuress; a mother gets a schoolmaster to beat her delinquent son; two housewives visit a temple and are shown round the works of art; a jealous mistress threatens her slave, whom she suspects of making love to another woman; and so on. Several of the mimes are more or less obscene. The skill lies in the naturalistic presentation of such material within a highly artificial dialect and an unusual metre. In the same period Aratus of Soli produced a versified account of the constellations, his *Phaenomena*. This is a sort of didactic poem, but unlike the work of Hesiod, Parmenides, or Empedocles (or the Latin Lucretius), it is not written in verse in order to convey a real message, the poet's own statement, but on the contrary exists to show how elegantly the poet can versify material already available in prose. The work is skilful and not without distinction; it had a great vogue, and it was translated into Latin by Cicero and again by Germanicus Caesar. Probably also writing about 260 B.C. was Lycophron of Chalcis. He was a scholar working at Alexandria, where he catalogued the works of the comic poets, and he achieved fame as a tragedian. His one surviving work, *Alexandra,* is a curious offshoot of tragedy. Raving Cassandra, the prophetic Trojan princess, delivers a tragic monologue of 1500 lines, in which the disasters which mythology has in store for the conquering Greeks, and the glories the future holds for the defeated Trojans, are prophetically unfolded in language of ferocious obscurity. It contains a remarkable prediction of the rise of Rome, which was beginning to make itself felt in the Aegean about this time.

III

We have now reviewed the poets of the first and greatest generation of Hellenistic poetry. They represent a remarkable range in subject and form, but all those whose work survives have in common a lively interest in perfection of form and sophistication of manner. They had many contemporaries whose aims were different, and who wrote more straightforward epics and hymns, but history was on the side of technique and craftsmanship. Two hundred years later they had a second heyday, in Rome; and again it was above all their technique which attracted the Latin poets, so that Catullus practised his skill by producing an exact translation (LXVI) of an elegy by Callimachus, and Virgil made his first published work an evocation of Theocritus. Their learning was such that from a very early date commentaries were produced on their poems, some of which we have on papyrus.

After Callimachus we can trace a decline of this school of poetry. The great scientist and polymath Eratosthenes, the first man to measure accurately the size of the earth, amused himself by writing verse in the Callimachean manner; he was Librarian of the Alexandrian Library. Euphorion of Chalcis, scholar and librarian, outdid his predecessors in the obscurity of the subjects and the language of his poetry. Nicander of Colophon, who apparently lived about 150 B.C., wrote many poems, of which we possess two, both in hexameters: *Theriaca,* on poisonous animals, and *Alexipharmaca,* on cures for poisons. The style is precious, the subjects repulsive, the information neither original nor reliable. At the end of the period, the tradition of Callimachus revives in Parthenius of Nicaea. Brought to Rome in 73 B.C. as a captive, he won his freedom and became highly influential on the Roman writers of his time. Virgil quotes a line of his verse in *Georgic* I, and he influenced Catullus and Cornelius Gallus, the inventor of Roman love-elegy, to whom his only extant work is addressed. No doubt he did much to fill Roman poets of the period with admiration for the Callimachean technique, and the desire to emulate it.

The second and first centuries B.C., with constant wars and the enormous destruction of the Greek world which accompanied the rise of Rome, were inauspicious for poetry. The Museum at Alexandria ceased to be a privileged place for scholars and poets in the middle of the second century, when in 145 they were expelled. Alexandria, though it had something of a revival in the first century, never again regained the intellectual standards of the early Ptolemaic period. In literature, as in science, it is impossible to evade the impression of a general decline: the energies of Hellenism were running down, and the harshness of Roman conquest and rule must have contributed heavily to this.

The only form which runs almost continuously through the period is the epigram. From the earliest period Greeks had inscribed on stone records of dedication of offerings to gods, epitaphs for the dead, and so on; by the fourth century poems were produced which were not really intended to be inscribed, and the epigram had become an independent form. Its conciseness made a special appeal to Hellenistic poets, almost all of whom are represented by extant examples. Often one poet produced a poem meant to be read as a variation on one already in existence — a procedure which is familiar to us in music rather than poetry. We are uniquely well supplied with this poetic form, thanks to the survival of the huge 'Palatine Anthology', which incorporates most of the anthology of epigrams formed by Meleager of Gadara under the title of 'The Garland', *c.*95 B.C. We thus possess well over 700 epigrams from this period, from the hands of more than 70 poets. It is possible here to do no more than mention a few of the more important.

Callimachus was a master of the form, as we should expect: his epigrams are inimitable in their neatness and point. He evokes but extends the reticence which forms such a great part of the charm of the archaic epitaphs:

> Here Dicon's son, Acanthian Saon, lies
> In holy sleep: say not, a good man dies.
> (Callimachus, *Epigrams* 9)

A number of his epigrams deal with love. Here is a typically subtle one; the scene is at a symposium, a drinking party, and as the toasts are drunk one of the company is unable to hide his feelings:

> Our friend there hides a wound. Did you espy
> The man's pathetic and deep-chested sigh
> At his third cup? And how the wreath he wore
> Dropped all its rosy petals on the floor?
> Properly smitten, that's my sworn belief;
> No guess-work — set a thief to catch a thief.
> (ibid. 43, translation R. A. Furness and G. M. Young)

Only in the last line does the poet hint that he, too, is in love, and not merely the sharp-eyed observer we were taking him for. Other epigrams versify some real episode:

> Cleombrotus called to the Sun 'Farewell!'
> And from a tower leapt down into hell.
> Not after deadly suffering, but he
> Read Plato's proof of immortality.
> (ibid. 23)

Another talented writer of epigrams of the same generation is Asclepiades; he was a lyric poet, but only his epigrams survive. He writes of love less indirectly than Callimachus, but can show a pleasing irony at his own expense:

> I'm tired of life, and not yet twenty-two:
> O gods of love, why burn me as you do?
> For if you kill me, where will be your sport?
> — You'll roll your dice, of course, without a thought.
> (*Palatine Anthology* xii 46)

Other poets who deal with love and wine are Posidippus and the collector of the Anthology, Meleager, who included more than a hundred of his own epigrams. His own work is rather more lush than the earlier poets; many of his poems have eight or ten lines, and he likes repetition. Some of them are in their own way fine, and come nearer than most Greek poetry to sounding, in the modern sense, romantic. Other poets specialized in epitaphs, sometimes moving. Here is one by Leonidas of Tarentum (*c.*250 B.C.):

> 'Like an old vine I'm forced to use a crutch;
> Calling me down I hear the voice of death —
> "Gorgus, give ear; it would not profit much
> For three or four more springs to draw your breath." '
> So spoke old Gorgus, meaning what he said,
> And spurning life went over to the dead.
>
> > (ibid. viii 731).

The poetess Anyte of Tegea, Leonidas, and others cultivated a tradition of the epigram which dealt with the events of simple lives — shepherds, fishermen, sailors — in language of artful complexity. The resemblance to Theocritus is obvious. Many of these poems have been written as if they could be inscribed as actual epitaphs or records of dedication to the gods, but that is only a form; in reality they are pure poetry.

Highly characteristic of the Hellenistic period is the new position of philosophy. Once Athens had delighted to see Socrates mocked by Aristophanes, and had in the end condemned him to death; but when in 155 an Athenian embassy had to be sent to Rome, it seemed natural to send the heads of the Academy, of the Peripatetics (the school of Aristotle), and of the Stoics. Every cultured man had an interest in philosophy, which came to be conceived of in terms of the separate schools. The schools continued to exist side by side, arguing with each other, for centuries. This tradition of philosophy captured the intellectual class of Rome and affected the early Church; by way of Lucretius, Cicero, Horace, Seneca, and Marcus Aurelius, and of Fathers such as Augustine, it was to have an effect on Europe for many centuries. Still in the eighteenth century its influence was powerful, in Pope and Swift and the writers of the Enlightenment.

Epicurus (*c.*341–270 B.C.) founded his school at Athens in

307/6. The aim of his doctrine is individual happiness, which he saw as menaced above all by fears and anxieties about the supernatural, superstition, fear of pain, fear of death. These can be dispelled, and to do so is the sole purpose of philosophy: 'that philosopher's teaching is futile who does not treat some passion; philosophy which does not expel passions from the soul is as useless as medicine which does not expel diseases from the body.' To this end he constructed an elaborate theory of physics, drawing on the speculations of Democritus in the fifth century, in which all things were the random creation of atoms and the void. This system could, of course, not be proved, but Epicurus regarded it as providing an explanation of the structure of things which was compatible with material data, and was also psychologically comforting in that it did away with the need for divine causation and any form of teleology. In literature it is most familiar to us from Lucretius' great poem, *De rerum natura*.

But the main point of Epicureanism was the life of rational pleasure and serenity. Epicurus was a man of personal magnetism, who attracted devoted disciples. 'Friendship' (or perhaps better 'affection') 'is the greatest of the things which wisdom provides for the happiness of one's whole life', was a doctrine of his; and the Epicureans were a society of friends, which admitted women and slaves on equal terms. All animals desire pleasure from birth, and it is the natural goal; this meant physical as well as mental pleasure. Many were shocked by the idea, so that 'Epicurean' came to be 'epicure', but the founder's own tastes were austere — he claimed to be happy with bread and water, and to regard cheese as a luxury — and he regarded the best form of pleasure as that which consisted not in change but in a steady state of tranquillity and freedom from pain. This was in fact the state which Epicurus ascribed to the gods, who were serene and happy but did nothing.

Epicurus virtually invented the philosophical letter (in this serving as a model for Horace and Seneca). We possess three important letters, which in warmth and tone rather resemble early Christian writings; the form enabled him to express his doctrine in a way which also expressed his friendships. He reduced his teachings to a catechism of forty propositions, and again to a 'fourfold medicine' which could be constantly present in the mind of the simplest disciple: 'God is not to be feared, death is not to be distrusted, what is good is easy to get, what is terrible is easy to endure.'

Such a doctrine made for a sort of egotism. Virtue itself is only good because it conduces to one's own happiness; as for society, the wise man will not enter public life if he can avoid it, and in general he will 'live unnoticed', in Epicurus' phrase. The attractiveness of the doctrine, which continued more or less unchanged for 500 years, was partly this passive sense of being put out of the power of external events and forces, happy in the kingdom of oneself, and partly it lay in the more positive sense of gratitude which it inculcated; gratitude towards life for the pleasures it provided — 'pleasure for a limited time is equal to pleasure for an infinite time,' says Epicurus, 'provided you measure its limits in the light of reason', so that the wise man becomes like a god and is as happy as a god.

The rival dogmatic school of the Stoa was founded by Zeno (*c.*332–261), who started teaching at Athens about 300 B.C. While we possess important documents from Epicurus' own hand, we have none of Zeno's works, nor do any of the voluminous treatises of the early Stoa survive. Yet the importance of the school obliges us to give a summary account of it. Zeno, like Epicurus, addressed himself to the question of individual happiness; his system, too, would make it possible for a man to be independent of external events, secure in his own happiness and virtue. But his approach was quite different. Instead of isolating the reasonable man within an essentially indifferent universe, the product of blind chance, and showing him how to satisfy a nature which, like that of the animals, aimed above all at pleasure, Zeno was impressed by the beauty and order of the world; such a cosmos could not be the result of chance but must be the work of an all-powerful Reason (Logos). This Logos, which he also called Providence and Destiny, runs through all things, human nature as well as the external world. The structure of the world and everything which happens in it follows a rational plan: human actions can be in accordance with it, too, if we have studied and understand it, and direct our will accordingly. 'God is immanent in matter, running through it all and arranging and shaping and making it into an ordered cosmos', so that Stoic theology has a pantheistic character. The psychological appeal of this doctrine is that it assures us that the world makes sense and is ordered for the best; we too are a part of this wonderful whole, and whatever happens to us is for the best. The Letters of Seneca and the work of Marcus Aurelius are for us the most approachable literary sources, from which we can see what an exhilaration this side of Stoic doctrine could convey.

What happens is determined from outside us, but the way in which we respond to it is crucial: 'Fate leads those who consent, but drags those who do not' — the difference is vital *to us*. Zeno's successor Cleanthes wrote Stoic poetry, some of which survives:

> Lead me, O Zeus and Destiny, where 'er
> It is my lot to go: most willingly
> I follow. But if I withhold consent
> Ignobly, I shall follow none the less.

He also is the author of a *Hymn to Zeus,* which attempts to combine the traditional forms of poetical prayer with the new complexities of Stoic doctrine.

The Stoa believed that man was not an isolated creature but a member of a community; while the Epicureans said that the wise man would not take part in public affairs unless obliged to, the Stoics said that he would unless he was prevented. Its less human side came from the single-minded insistence that only virtue is good, such things as health, position, pleasure, being 'indifferent', and that all emotions were bad (emotion is defined as 'irrational and unnatural movement of the soul'). The wise man is as far from feeling pity as he is from feeling envy; and 'just as you drown as surely when one inch under water as on the bottom', so every act which fails even by a little to be perfect is bad, every man who fails to be perfectly wise is a fool. Wise men are very rare; therefore virtually all men are bad, incapable of a truly good action.

The paradoxical nature of these doctrines ensured that they were constantly attacked. Stoics and Epicureans, with dogmas to defend, were opposed by Sceptics and by the Academy, which after Arcesilaus (315–240) was devoted to criticism of dogmatic assertions — a return to the tradition of Socrates. Chrysippus, who is said to have written more than 700 volumes, embedded

Stoicism in a massive stronghold of logic; its doctrines were later humanized by Panaetius and Posidonius.

Panaetius, an aristocrat and a man of the world, turned Stoic rigidity into a code for a gentleman: not *all* emotion, but only *excessive* emotion, was to be condemned; and the black-and-white contrast of absolute right and absolute wrong was developed into an elaborate system of rational duties, represented for us by Cicero's *De Officiis*. He was intimate with Scipio Aemilianus, and his thought did much to offer a code of values to the Roman aristocracy, who in conquering the world had outgrown their own old simple values and badly needed a new set, which for men who had discovered Greek culture had to have a Greek intellectual backing. Posidonius (*c.*135–50 B.C.) is one of the most interesting figures of the Hellenistic period. He too impressed powerful Romans, including Pompey and Cicero. He was a great traveller and observer, recording with gusto and lively style both natural and social phenomena; and a writer on many subjects — history, ethnography, geography, physics, ethics, psychology, literary criticism. He attempted to reunite history with philosophy by showing that an universal 'sympathy' connected everything in the world. The movements of the tides, the adjustment of animals to the seasons, plants coming to life on the day of the Winter Solstice, all formed a cosmos whose remotest parts were all connected; one 'vital force' ran through all things, from stones to men. Gravity was to be explained as the earth attracting to itself things which naturally belonged to it, while the writer of universal history was a 'sort of minister of Divine Providence', making a single orderly narrative out of events, as God makes an orderly system of the heavenly bodies and also of the natures of men.

The only great historian whose work largely survives is Polybius. The early histories of Alexander's conquests, like the melodramatic productions of the 'tragic' historians whom Polybius criticizes, are almost completely lost. Polybius of Megalopolis (200–118 B.C.) composed an ambitious History, which originally was meant to show how in 53 years, from 219 to 167 B.C., Rome conquered almost the whole world, an unprecedented achievement. He had a political career at home until he was taken to Rome as a hostage in 167 (the hostages were detained there until 151), and is scornful of historians who are merely bookish; real experience, action, and travel are vital if one is to understand political events. But he also worked in Roman archives, and was praised by Cicero for his knowledge of Roman matters. Above all he was an intimate of Scipio Aemilianus, the most powerful man of his time, whom he accompanied on several campaigns. Conversation with leading Romans was an important source for his work.

Polybius is very explicit in discussing his views and intentions in writing history. His work is meant to be practically useful to the man of action, explaining how and why things happen. And it is an universal history, for the rise of Rome has made history no longer a plurality of separable narratives; every part of the known world is involved with every other. Greeks found it hard to accept their subjection to the culturally inferior Romans; Polybius explains how it has happened — not by mere chance, but because of the superiority of the Roman constitution and system, and of the moral qualities they produced. In book vi of his *History* he gives a valuable account of Rome from this point of view. His style is generally bureaucratic and unattractive, but there are lively passages (for example xxxi 12ff., Demetrius' escape from Rome); and he can be pathetic (xxxix 2, the sack of Corinth). After 168 he decided, in the light of events, to carry his work down to 146, when Rome destroyed the great cities of Carthage and Corinth, and the world was left in no doubt at all that Roman power and domination were absolute and inescapable.

His standpoint is realistic; at moments indeed, his dispassionate account of Roman harshness seems cynical, especially in the latter books; often he is content to let terrible events speak for themselves. He is a very intelligent writer, and though he does not convey the same sense of intellectual power as Thucydides, nor the charm of Herodotus, his cool understanding and insight entitle him to be called a great historian.

The period which we have been discussing was one in which writers who had something new to say to the world were likely to write in prose, but from which the surviving literary work is largely in verse. Many long poems were still composed in conventional styles and modes, but the poetry which survives was written on a small scale, in a style witty, learned, and unhackneyed. Sensibility and even sentimentality begin to come in, and the English reader is reminded at some moments of the Metaphy-sical poets, at others of the 1890s. The vast scale of universal histories and the great range of technical works, both scientific and scholarly, were accompanied at the opposite pole, in poetry and philosophy, by a turning inwards to the individual self. A growing interest in the cultivation or the repression of one's own emotions, like an interest in the remote and the enormous, was a consequence of the eclipse of the old city states, narrow but intense, by the great empires and federations of the new world.

10 Greek literature after 50 B.C.

I

The expansion of Roman power which gave Polybius his theme continued in the century following the destruction of Corinth in 146 B.C. Some Greek kingdoms passed peacefully into Rome's control, but others required force of arms, while even greater havoc was wreaked in the Greek cities of the eastern Mediterranean by the succession of Roman civil wars in the first century B.C. Antony's defeat by Octavian at Actium in 31 B.C. at last brought peace to the Greek world, already even in its exhausted condition the culturally dominant component of Rome's empire. Egypt, realm of Antony's Ptolemaic ally Cleopatra and last of the great Hellenistic monarchies, was annexed in the following year. In the succeeding century the remaining territories of the Levant, territories whose educated language was Greek, slipped one by one from the status of client kingdom to that of Roman province. The last annexation of significance was that of Commagene on the Euphrates frontier in A.D. 72: it is symptomatic of the diffusion of Hellenism in the Roman empire that this tiny and peripheral country was shortly to give birth to the period's most entertaining writer, Lucian (see below p. 168).

Civil wars in the years following A.D. 68 and A.D. 192 and recurrent frontier wars with Parthia caused some Greek cities distress. But overall the three centuries following Actium were tranquil and prosperous, a favourable climate for the maturing of Hellenistic into Graeco-Roman culture. Cities recovered from the ravages of conquest and civil war. By the second century A.D. Athens, in Cicero's day a pathetic shadow of her former self, was again a cultural capital of the Greek world. Her libraries and professors promoted literary activity. On the west coast of Asia Minor she had rivals in Pergamum, Smyrna, and Ephesus, and the cultural centre of gravity returned from Alexandria to the Aegean. But everywhere the veneer of Hellenism spread by

Alexander's conquests was growing thicker. The Romans encouraged the growth of cities, and new foundations can be traced in their hundreds where before there had only been villages. With cities went education — at secondary level in established literary classics, at tertiary in rhetoric and philosophy. A system elaborated partly to ensure that Greeks stayed Greek now dispensed the social asset of Greek language and culture to Phrygians, Cappadocians, and Syrians: hence grew a reading public of unprecedented size, eager for entertainment that was fashionable and erudition that could be flaunted. Not surprisingly there was a vast literary output, much of it from experts in rhetoric or philosophy.

As in the Hellenistic period, hundreds of writers are known to us by name and little more. But far more writing, particularly in prose, has survived from the first four centuries of our era than from the previous three, and our scores of complete texts can be augmented by Byzantine quotations and epitomes. Much that has come down is second-rate, and it is a reasonable conjecture that what is lost was mostly worse rather than better. But some authors we can read stand comparison with the classical period and justify the frequent characterization of the second and third centuries A.D. as a renaissance.

One feature that has encouraged this term is the very return to classical models. Imitation of the vocabulary and style of Attic orators of the fourth century B.C., 'Atticism', took hold first in oratory and spread to other genres. When Dionysius, a teacher of rhetoric from Halicarnassus, came to Rome in 30 B.C. the exuberant language and rhythms branded as 'Asianist' by their opponents were already — to his delight — out of fashion. In writing his essay *On Imitation* and his perceptive studies of ancient orators — Lysias, Isocrates, Isaeus, and Demosthenes — he was preaching to the converted, at least in Rome. When the renaissance began in the late first century A.D., the language of Plato, Xenophon, and the orators was the norm for literary Greek, and the spoken language — the *koinē* — was tolerated only for technical and sub-literary purposes. But imitation of fourth-century Athens went further. The Platonic dialogue became a favourite literary form. The works of Xenophon were also imitated (most extensively by Arrian, who actually took the name

Xenophon) and his *Cyropaedia* even influenced the novel.

A few sensitive spirits saw that imitation could only create good literature if it focused broadly on mood and approach and not narrowly on detail. But detail was easier to master. By the middle of the second century practitioners of display oratory argued about the attestation of Attic words, lexica were compiled to define accepted usage (one of those to survive is Phrynichus' *Selection*), and Aristophanes' comedies were read more for their vocabulary than their humour. Since all education involved rhetoric, and since teachers of rhetoric turned their hand to many branches of literature, most writing shows the effect of this Atticism. A typical product is the collection of twenty letters by Aelian purporting to be the correspondence of Attic farmers in appropriately pure dialect. His early third century A.D. readers will have enjoyed noting the influence of Attic comedy on his rural vignettes and admired the arch simplicity of thought and language.

Such writing is part of a wider attempt by Greeks of the Roman empire to recreate a past when they were their own political masters. Many writers betray no hint of the Roman empire or of the presence of Roman soldiers and administrators in the eastern Mediterranean, and rarely do we encounter knowledge of Latin literature. Yet the Latin west was a vital factor in the Greek renaissance. Rome joined eastern cities as a centre of Greek culture, attracting and even producing Greek writers — Aelian was a native of the Latin city of Praeneste (Palestrina). Cultivated Latins from Italy, and soon from Spain, Africa, and Gaul, venerated the Greek literary heritage. Latin writing emulated it, and it must have been as unusual for a Latin writer not to know Greek as it was for a Greek writer to display a knowledge of Latin. As Greeks entered the Roman administration and Italian settlers in Greek lands became Hellenized, there developed an integrated Graeco-Roman upper class that in many respects shared a common culture. Westerners like Suetonius, Fronto, and Marcus Aurelius wrote in both languages. Yet not until the late fourth century do we find Greeks — Ammianus Marcellinus and Claudian — who chose Latin for a literary work. Joint acceptance of Greek as the senior language and literature is one factor, but the doctrine of imitation and the hankering to live in a pre-

Roman world must also have been important in immunizing
Greek literature against Latin influence.

II

Historiography exemplifies many features of the period. No new
forms or approaches were developed. Herodotus, Thucydides,
and Ephorus were retained as models, although some, like
Arrian, preferred Xenophon: but only occasionally was contemporary history essayed. In rehashing history of the more or less
distant past there was no room for personal observation, and
historians' investigations were conducted in libraries, comparing
accounts of their predecessors and then often adhering to one
alone for long sections of narrative. The search for truth was not
forgotten, but its discovery naturally became less dramatic, and
for many writers style was of equal if not greater moment.

Such a historian was Dionysius of Halicarnassus, already
mentioned as a critic. His assessments of the orators and the
criticisms advanced in his monograph on Thucydides are primarily stylistic. But he saw that what was said was as important as
how it was said and that there was an essential connection
between these aspects of a writer's work. Admittedly his complaints about Thucydides' subject-matter and arrangement are
as unconvincing as those about his style are trenchant. But he
was genuinely interested in the writing of history, and in 8 B.C.
published *The Early History of Rome* in twenty books. Much
research seems to have gone into the surviving ten books, which
often offer a useful control on Livy's account: but the rhetori-
cian's hand is everywhere apparent, and the Greek with Roman
friends and domicile allowed himself to present the Romans
themselves as Greek in their origins.

Only fragments remain of the forty-seven-book Roman history
by his contemporary Strabo (*c*.64 B.C.–? A.D. 24). From the period
covered, the late republic, and from Strabo's surviving seventeen-
book geography, we can judge that we have lost an important
work in the tradition of Polybius, whose narrative he took up.
Strabo too came from Asia Minor — Amasia near the Black Sea
— and spent much of his life in Rome. He accompanied a prefect

of Egypt on an expedition to Arabia, and many comments in his geography — such as his note of the economic arguments against attempting to annex Britain — show a hard-headed ability to see things from a Roman point of view. He thought his work should be useful and directed it particularly to politicians. But he, too, took literary tradition seriously. Homer is his starting-point and much space is occupied in the geography by polemic against Eratosthenes.

For the hundred years following the geography's publication in A.D. 24 Greek historical writing is represented for us by the *Jewish War* and *Jewish Antiquities* of Josephus (*c.*A.D. 35–95). Despite Jewish authorship and theme, the works are very much in the Greek tradition in a way that later Christian histories like Eusebius' *History of the Church* are not. Indeed Josephus' account of Vespasian's suppression of the Jewish revolt is the only war monograph on the pattern of Thucydides' history to survive from the period.

A very different perspective moulded the historical work of Arrian (*c.*A.D. 90–170). From Nicomedia in Bithynia (N.W. Asia Minor), he may owe to the friendship of Hadrian his entry to the Roman senate and rise to the consulate, but his own talents were manifestly diverse. An elegant dedicatory epigram has recently been discovered from his term as governor of Bactica in Southern Spain. While governing Cappadocia he not only repelled a barbarian invasion but wrote up the campaign in restrained and terse Greek, referring to himself as Xenophon. He was already known as a philosopher, and his publication of the *Lectures of Epictetus* in twelve books (cf. below p. 172) evoked Xenophon's *Recollections of Socrates*. To Xenophon's city Athens he retired in the 140s and used the classical author's *Anabasis* as model for his own *Anabasis* ('Journey to the Interior') *of Alexander*.

The historical importance of the *Anabasis* is a function of our loss of other full and reliable accounts. But as it is we can be grateful that Arrian chose good sources, Ptolemy and Aristobulus, and is prepared to distinguish their versions from 'the tradition' at large. He is not so systematic in this as he promises and as we would wish; he makes mistakes, and his enthusiasm for his hero sometimes warps his judgement. But it is not mere rhetorical history. Arrian tries to get things right, and the restrained economy of presentation and low-key Xenophontic style make for very readable narrative. In an age when boasts were the coin of literary exchanges we need not sneer at Arrian's self-confidence:

But this I would record, that to me this literary activity *is* my country and family and public offices, and has been right from my youth. And on this account I think myself not unworthy of the first rank in Greek letters, just indeed as Alexander was of the first rank in arms.

(Arrian, *Anabasis* i 12.5)

Arrian moved on to other themes — the chaos on Alexander's death and the history of Rome's dealings with Parthia. Loyal to his native land, he also eventually published, after lifelong research, a history of Bithynia. These witnesses to his wide historical range are sadly lost.

For Appian, too, a barrister from Alexandria whose career took him to Rome and ultimately the rank of procurator, his own province of origin was important. To him the Ptolemies were 'my kings'. The organization of his twenty-four-book history of Rome, published *c.*A.D. 160, shows the influence of Herodotus and a provincial perspective. He judged that traditional annalistic treatments impeded coherent assessment of Rome's dealings with nations she conquered and of either side's virtues: hence he took the conquered as focal points, allocating each a book in the order of its first encounter with Rome. Some themes called for different treatment. The first book embraced the regal period; one dealt with each of Rome's great foes, Hannibal and Mithridates; Egypt was given four, alas now lost. Five narrate the civil wars of late republican Rome, linked to Appian's theme by their culmination in Egypt's annexation, and are our only continuous account of the period from the Gracchi to Augustus. Their narrative is usually reliable and often exciting. Appian chose a good source and his own writing can be concise, lucid, and vigorous. His language, like his extensive use of speeches, shows the influence of classical historians, but it avoids the extremes of Atticism, even admitting Roman technical terms in transliteration.

Cassius Dio (*c.*A.D. 160–235) shares with Arrian — whose biography he wrote — Bithynian origins and a Roman senatorial career. But he came to history a different way. Successful monographs on the portents and then on the wars that ushered in the Severan dynasty encouraged him to undertake a full history of Rome. Its eighty books ended with his own second consulate in A.D. 229 and required ten years of research followed by twelve of writing. Although much survives only in Byzantine epitome even this preserves important historical material. For the period within his own lifetime Dio's career allowed him to record vivid details and form useful judgements. His views may also be detected in the speeches, of which the best-known is the pair given to Agrippa and Maecenas advocating republic and monarchy respectively. But neither here nor in narrative does his writing rise above the pedestrian, and it is for his historical and not his literary contribution that he is to be valued.

His contemporary Herodian had higher literary ambitions. The Thucydidean model for his eight books on the bellicose years from A.D. 180 to 238, emphasized by verbal echoes, arouses hopes of good history, too: but these are soon dashed. Although Herodian can claim to have witnessed some of what he narrates or to have questioned men who did, his account is unreliable and unbalanced, geared more to rhetorical effect than establishing the truth.

Herodian was not the last Greek historian to feel Thucydides' power. When the Heruli invaded Greece in A.D. 267 and sacked Athens, the man who encouraged the Athenians to battle with reminders of their past, Herennius Dexippus, wrote a Thucydidean account of the war that we have unfortunately lost. Still later, in the sixth century, both Thucydides and Herodotus influenced Procopius' *Wars*. They are but two of many constituents of the Greek tradition that survived the demise of the truly classical world.

III

History proper was not the only genre to show such influence. Much in Pausanias' *Guide to Greece*, published *c.*A.D. 180, recalls Herodotus, even if he lacks Herodotus' elegance and historical perspective. Pausanias does not limit himself to dry descriptions of shrines and secular monuments, but balances these with legendary and historical anecdotes which still make his work a rewarding travelling companion. Despite his frequent recourse to written sources rather than autopsy, Pausanias' account of Greece's monumental centres at their fullest extent is invaluable, not merely to archaeologists, but to anyone who tries to envisage the material surroundings of classical antiquity. His interest in things sacred is also a good index of the religious temper of his age.

A century earlier another man whose work moved on the frontiers of historiography had shown similar antiquarian and religious interests, Plutarch of Chaeronia (*c.*A.D. 40–?120). Of all the Greek writers of the empire Plutarch is deservedly the most read. He attracts us by his humanity, his lack of pretension, and his infectious interest in almost any area of intellectual activity. He compels our attention by his vast knowledge of his classical heritage, a heritage which he seems often to see from the point of view of a modern reader, and by the extent to which his interpretation of that heritage illuminates the preoccupations of his own age. Rome and Romans were well known to him. His patrons included leading senators like Sosius Senecio, to whom the *Lives* are dedicated. No difference is apparent in his attitude to Greek and Roman friends, yet Plutarch is through and through a Greek. Rather than reside in Italy he chose to stay in the small town of his birth 'lest it become smaller', and from an essay on how to run a Greek city under the eye of Roman governors we know he involved himself in the detailed execution of its public works. Delphi, too, renascent in an age of tourism and religiosity, benefited from his participation and is the setting for some of his dialogues. Yet the important element in his life, the seal of his Hellenism, to which the active life was only a frame, was talking and teaching, reading, thinking, and writing.

If labels were compulsory then Plutarch would have to be classified as a philosopher. He taught philosophy and a large group of his essays are on moral philosophy — hence the essays' collective title *Moralia*. But although he is versed in all the technical arguments of the major schools and can enter the arid debates of Stoic logic, he stands out as a natural moral teacher. Sense and sensibility win over the reader to his way of seeing actions or situations. His essays on *Garrulousness, Checking Anger,* or *Keeping up your Spirits* can still help readers to a happier life. Plutarch patiently accumulates arguments, sketches out images which may illustrate by contrast or comparison, and sprinkles the mixture liberally with quotations from the poets. His thoughts seem to develop naturally, flooding into swollen and tortuous periods, often hard to follow but a welcome change from the mannered balance of his contemporary display orators. His advice on listening to lectures is a fair sample:

So you ought to set aside the superfluous and vacuous element of style and go for the actual fruit, following the example not of women who weave garlands but of bees. For the women make for plants with fine flowers and scents and plait them, weaving a product that is pleasing but ephemeral and fruitless: but the bees often fly past meadows of violets, roses, and hyacinths and land on what is sharpest and most pungent, thyme — there they settle down, 'their thoughts on golden honey' [Simonides] and fly off with something that is useful for their specific activity. So too, then, the professional and committed student ought to pass over flowery and luxuriant language and dramatic and pompous themes, dismissing them as the fodder of sophistic drones, and plunge his attention into the meaning of the lecture and the approach of the lecturer, drawing from it what is useful and beneficial, remembering that he has come not to a theatre or concert-hall but to a place of learning and instruction, with the intention of putting his life right by the lecture.

(Plutarch, *On listening to lectures* 41E–42A)

But this is not Plutarch's only side. Other essays show his deep interest in questions of science, religion, or history. It is the historian and the moralist that combine in the *Parallel Lives*. A sequence of Lives of the Roman emperors (of which only *Galba* and *Otho* survive) had already shown his interest in Roman historical biography. Then, in his later years, he wrote the great series of twenty-three pairs of parallel Greek and Roman biographies that has so strongly moulded the modern world's conceptions of their subjects, and indeed our tacit assumptions about who the major figures of classical antiquity were and what a biography should be. For Plutarch, biography's difference from history lay in its focus on character:

... it is not histories I am writing but lives; and in the most glorious deeds there is not always an indication of virtue or vice, indeed a small thing like a phrase or a jest often makes a greater revelation of a character than battles where thousands die . . .

(Plutarch, *Alexander* c. 1)

Not that Plutarch is negligible as a historian: the *Lives* often present a clear and valuable narrative. But the reader is meant to learn from the subject's choices and reactions set against the moving backdrop of momentous history. The pairing of Greek and Roman statesmen should perhaps be taken as a testimony to how Plutarch thought the two cultures might be seen rather than proof that his age already saw them as equal partners. Within the *Lives* little stress is laid on specifically Greek or Roman traits. Background, education, and friendships are seen as important influences, and the interplay between character and external circumstances is followed through in narrative that exploits irony, tension, and changes of pace. Plutarch's medium allows him to select incidents most illustrative of his hero's moral biography and to colour them to suit his interpretation. His eye for telling detail and skill in anecdote absorb our attention in his story and engage our sympathies with his protagonist.

IV

Biography of a very different sort survives from the pen of the Athenian Philostratus. Towards A.D. 230 he published eight books on the ascetic guru Apollonius of Tyana, credited by tradition with utterances and miracles comparable to those attributed to his near-contemporary Jesus of Nazareth. Philostratus' historical novel went further, presenting Apollonius as a Pythagorean whose search for wisdom took him to India and Ethiopia and whose visits to Rome brought him into conflict with Nero and Domitian. His pseudo-Socratic conversations reflect many of the intellectual preoccupations of Philostratus' own time, especially the move of philosophy towards mysticism. The work itself is an interesting experiment, drawing on the structure and themes of the erotic novel (cf. below p. 170) to add bulk and charm to hagiography, a form familiar at many literary levels but always on a smaller scale.

Philostratus was himself a sophist, a display orator, and his

Lives of the Sophists are also interesting both for form and content. Unlike such compilations of *Lives* in a more or less scholarly tradition as Diogenes Laertius' *Lives of Philosophers,* Philostratus' two books are artistically arranged. A long life of Polemo of Laodicea at the end of the first balances that of Herodes Atticus opening the second, and the sixty-odd shorter lives furnish a sort of pedimental framework. Moreover, the sequence is nothing less than a history of the 'Second Sophistic', the development of display oratory into a major cultural activity, traced by Philostratus to the late first century A.D. and seen by him as a continuation of the classical sophists' involvement in the teaching and demonstration of rhetoric. At a time when there was no political history of the Greek cities to write, this account of their most prestigious cultural figures may be attempting to offer an alternative.

Speeches which gave an opportunity to display skill in praise or blame were a feature of Greek oratory from the start. They were needed for some public occasions (for example, funeral speeches at Athens) and could be used by a professional like Gorgias to show off his talents. But speeches of persuasion for the courtroom and assembly were valued higher by posterity, and in the Hellenistic period students of rhetoric composed speeches for imaginary court cases and for imaginary assemblies, sometimes assuming what had been real historical situations. By the late first century A.D. public displays, especially of this latter type of speech, had become a major art form. Established or visiting teachers of rhetoric would draw a crowd of critical but potentially enthusiastic connoisseurs. We know from Philostratus that brilliance of language and delivery were as important as ingenuity of argument. Bold conceits or striking rhythms might draw applause, perhaps prompted by a claque of pupils, whereas one speaker purporting to speak *ex tempore* on a theme proposed from the floor — this too being a popular form — was discomfited by a rival's fan-club chanting out in unison with him the words they knew he had in fact rehearsed. A successful sophist commanded the adulation now reserved for a *prima donna* or pop star, and often behaved similarly. However, most sophists came from the leading families of their city. In real life they spoke in debates, represented the city's interests on embassies and delivered speeches at dedications of temples. Their activity as sophists brought them privileges from the Roman government and, for a few, secured entry to an administrative career. But a political leader in Ephesus or Smyrna might well find his ambitions for his city checked by a Roman governor, and it is understandable that he should enjoy setting his display speeches in a fantasy world of Greek autonomy and present himself as Demosthenes outwitting Philip of Macedon.

Much sophistic oratory survives, and in its penumbra we find several literary forms whose chief common factor is that they were composed by sophists and intended for live performance to an alert audience. We cannot share the enthusiasm of the audiences described by Philostratus: Greek drama is performed in scores of languages and styles, but nobody, as far as I know, has tried to re-enact a sophistic display. Yet we must recognize the intellectual energy that was channelled into the art: although some of its features — like imitation of both language and situations of the classical period — encouraged derivative and uninspired writing, there were also attempts at development which in the hands of a man like Lucian produced new and worthwhile creations.

The first sophist of whom we can form a rounded impression is Dio of Prusa (*c.*A.D. 45–110) whom posterity nicknamed 'Golden-mouthed' (*Chrysostomos*). His refutation of the Homeric account of the Trojan War is a typical display of the power of argument. But we also have speeches made by Dio on real occasions, examples of political in-fighting in Prusa or statesmanlike advocacy of restraint to cities in his own and other Greek provinces disrupted by mutual competitiveness or internal dissensions. Dio was also a philosopher — a role he attributed to exile under Domitian — and four works on kingship (two of which were delivered to Trajan) are a serious attempt to apply theories of monarchy to the situation of the Roman emperor. Two are in dialogue form — Alexander debates with Philip, Diogenes with Alexander — and its exploitation in many of his seventy-odd works is to be explained by his philosophical *persona*. The *Charidemus* even has a pair of Platonic myths allegorizing the condition of man, and its power and charm recalls Plato's *Phaedo,* a work Dio so admired that he took a copy into exile.

Other dialogues of Dio's are purely literary. The point of such works as his *Chryseis,* based on the first book of the *Iliad,* is simply to entertain by vivid reworking of a familiar scene. This exploitation of a form traditionally employed for philosophy — and occasionally, as by Plutarch, for investigating other topics of learned interest — constituted an important addition to the armoury of belles-lettres, soon to be perfected by Lucian. Another development of a literary weapon which goes back to Plato is seen in Dio's *Euboean Tale*: a novelistic sketch of idyllic pastoral life in backwoods Euboea, which Dio claims himself to have witnessed when shipwrecked, is used to introduce serious proposals for repatriating the urban proletariat to the countryside. The technique recalls Plato's myths, but Dio's narrative shares interesting features with that contemporary development of prose fiction, the ideal romance.

Dio has an undemanding style and a lighter side that can rise to humour. Very different is Aelius Aristides (A.D. 117–c.180). In his argumentative speeches, a high proportion of the fifty-three pieces to survive, his complex organization and elaborate periods make for difficult reading: his rehabilitation of the Demosthenic style impressed contemporaries and continued to influence oratory in the fourth century but contributed nothing new. We may find it easier to respond to the short, repeated phrases of his *Lament for Smyrna* after the devastating earthquake of 178, a work that moved the emperor Marcus to shed tears on his copy:

Now ought all the birds of the air to have plunged into the flames — for the city has these in abundance — and the whole continent to have shorn its hair — for its own prize lock has gone — now ought the rivers to have run with tears, now the merchantmen to have put to sea with black sails. O river Meles, flowing through a desert; o melodies with which I now respond to those I voiced before, o song of swans and chorus of nightingales . . .

(Aristides xviii 9)

The effects sought by such 'Asianic' rhetoric may seem to us more appropriate to poetry than prose. In another genre, too, Aristides applied baroque prose rhetoric to a traditionally poetic task, hymns to the gods, and in that to Sarapis (45K) defends the use of prose as a medium older and more natural than verse. It is an interesting recognition of the extent to which sophistic prose was self-consciously annexing many of the classical domains of poetry.

For Renaissance and modern readers the greatest sophistic writer is a man whom only one contemporary, the polymath doctor Galen, even mentions, and whom Philostratus probably scorned as a renegade: Lucian. From a town on the Euphrates, where most people spoke Aramaic, Lucian came to Ionia in the A.D. 140s to learn from its great sophists, and then went on tour in Asia Minor, Greece, Italy, and Gaul. His conventional sophistic pieces are competent and no more. But a gift for biting satire as well as elegant and easy-flowing Greek gave him confidence to compose a flood of witty essays and dialogues, works which exploit the techniques, and seem intended for the normal audiences, of sophistic speeches. Yet even in this innovation the classical heritage was important: Lucian acknowledges the influence of Platonic dialogue and of Old Comedy, and the debunking *persona* inherited from the latter is fortified by imitation of a Hellenistic writer, Menippus the Cynic, whom Lucian often introduces as a character in dialogues. Venerated types of intellectual are exposed as cranks and impostors — self-righteous philosophers, pedantic grammarians, vain sophists, and fraudulent prophets of new religions.

This satire has its serious side. Lucian claims to have passed through a philosophical phase, and his portraits of the Platonist Nigrinus, who opened his eyes to the vanity of worldly ambitions, and of the Stoic teacher Demonax have a ring of sincere admiration. Yet the simple life urged by speakers in his Menippean dialogues when they discredit wealth, honour, and power was hardly the life Lucian or his audience led. They may have felt better for listening to the preaching of an ideal they admired from afar, but the conspectus of Lucian's work suggests he aimed more to entertain and be applauded than to instruct. Some of his satire is at the expense not of real people but of figures familiar from mythology and history. The quiet wit of his miniature *Conversations* between gods or tarts draws smiles at his subtle manipulation of traditional images but hurts nobody:

ZEUS Asclepius . . . Heracles . . . stop bickering with each other. Just like *men*! It won't do; it's out of place in a gods' party.

HERACLES Look here, Zeus, are you prepared to have this potion-monger in a better seat than me?

ASCLEPIUS Of course — I *am* better after all.·

HERACLES What makes you better, you thunderstruck oaf? Is it that Zeus struck you with lightning when you were doing what you ought not to have done, and now he's made you an immortal out of pity?

ASCLEPIUS So — have you forgotten that you too were burned up by fire, Heracles, on Mount Oeta? Is that why you're taunting me with my fiery past?

(Lucian, Conversations of Gods 15.1)

In other works Lucian entertains by flights of fantasy rather than satire, most strikingly in the *True Stories,* a traveller's tale which takes the narrator inside a gigantic whale and up to the moon. In yet others he exploits his gift for story-telling for its own sake — the *Toxaris,* with ten tales of friendship, and *Liars,* with nine of magic and superstition. These works seem to be the nearest prose fiction came to the respectable salons of high literature.

V

Yet throughout this period, albeit neglected by contemporary critics and theorists, prose fiction on a larger scale was being written, often by rhetoricians, and avidly read. Lucian himself is probably the author of the Greek original of Apuleius' Latin *Golden Ass,* where the adventures of the narrator-turned-ass offer ample scope for magic, humour, and erotic incident. But the most popular form (to judge from five examples to survive complete and many fragments on papyrus) handled the basic ingredients of adventure and love in a more serious way. The 'ideal romance' was probably developed in the first century B.C. and our earliest example, Chariton's *Chaereas and Callirhoe,* seems already to be operating with recognized conventions. The plot remains standard in most of his successors. Boy and girl, enviably rich and beautiful, fall in love and are separated. Their adventures take them over much of the Levant and expose life and virtue to peril. Despite near misses they survive chaste to be reunited and live happily ever after.

Such is the Greek novel. It betrays the influence of earlier literature, most obviously the *Odyssey* and New Comedy (see

Chapter 5). But although it may be intended for the same market that these genres had once satisfied, it is in no sense a development of them, and bears many hallmarks of the era in which it was fashioned. The characters are recognizably members of the educated élite of contemporary Greek cities — even Chaereas and Callirhoe, whom their author portrays as historical figures of the fifth century B.C. In two of the novels (those of Xenophon and Achilles) the stage is explicitly the Graeco-Roman world of the eastern Mediterranean, more infested with robbers and pirates than in most periods of the Roman peace: even the ostensibly classical setting offered by Chariton and Heliodorus assumes the boundaries of the Roman empire, and the tale has to move beyond them to Persia or Ethiopia for an extra frisson of the unknown. As in bourgeois city life, morality and religion are taken seriously, and the reader's cultural tastes are well served by good classical Greek, echoes and quotations of classical writers, and debates or digressions on varied topics of contemporary interest. This last trait is most prominent in Achilles and Heliodorus, who probably wrote latest of the authors to survive, and it may be that their baroque elaboration of a form which in the hands of Chariton was simple though sophisticated is at once evidence that the genre's capacity for development was limited and the fatal touch that secured its extinction.

Novelty could, of course, be secured by variations within the standard plot. Chariton's couple are married before a separation that lasts eight books, Achilles' lovers elope together and on separation only the heroine remains chaste. For linear narrative Heliodorus substitutes a complex sequence of flashback, subplots, and even false tales. But despite frequent focus on the principals' emotions their characters are never built up as in the novel's modern descendants: this opening for development was either inconceivable or neglected, and only one writer, Longus, gives a major role to the growth of the young people's love.

Longus (*c*.A.D. 200) is original in other ways too. Instead of far-flung cities and exotic lands the scene is the Aegean island of Lesbos; Daphnis and Chloe lead the life of simple shepherds. Longus exploits their idyllic environment and charming naïveté to present a rare vision of humanity in tune with nature. The gradual burgeoning of their passion is marked by the advance of the seasons. Interruptions there must be — a rival cowherd and kidnappings by pirates and invaders. But interventions by country deities — Pan, the Nymphs, and Eros — save the couple and the way is prepared for their ultimate union by instruction in the theory of love from old Philetas and in its practice by an older woman's seduction of Daphnis. In a skilful dénouement their aristocratic parentage is discovered and they return from their city families to a honeymoon and happy future in the country.

Longus' extensive use of short, balanced phrases and dislike of complex periods suits his pictorial mode and the simplicity of his characters:

What can it be that Chloe's kiss is doing to me? Her lips are gentler than roses and her mouth sweeter than honeycombs, but her kiss is sharper than a bee's sting. Often have I kissed kids, often have I kissed new-born puppies and the calf which was a present from Dorco: but this kiss is something new. My breath leaps up, my heart bounds up, my soul melts — and yet I want to kiss again. O harsh victory! O strange disease, whose name I cannot even say . . .

(Longus, *Daphnis and Chloe* i 18)

Such prose seems to us poetic, and indeed much in Longus' themes and expression derives from earlier poetry. The range of subjects and styles being attempted by prose partly explains the virtual absence of good poetry from the first three centuries A.D. Not that poetry was not written. Everywhere elegiac couplets were written for inscriptions and as literary epigrams. Crinagoras (late first century B.C.) is as clever as his Hellenistic predecessors at exploiting the epigram's capacity for pointed wit:

In all Menander's many roles you played,
Your brilliance proved a Muse's or a Grace's aid.
(*Palatine Anthology* ix 513)

This epitaph for an actor is not untypical of pieces by poets who were good enough to have their poems collected and anthologized in antiquity. But in every Greek community such elegiac couplets were in use until the sixth century for epitaphs, and many by unnamed poets are of fair quality; like this one from Rome:

Chelidon, acolyte of Zeus, whose skill for years
Was tending altars of my deity,

By children blessed I lie, and ask not tears:
The heavens surely saw my piety.
                    (*GVI* 566)

The purely literary epigram could also be used for satire, as by Argentarius (first century A.D.):

I loved a lass Alcippe, and my plea
Once coaxed her furtively to share my bed;
Both hearts beat fast, lest someone come and see
The goal to which our secret longings led;
The creaking springs betrayed us; suddenly there
Her mother stood, saying 'Lucky finds we share'.
                    (*Palatine Anthology* v 126)

Attractive as such poems are, they offer nothing new. Nor did hexameter poetry. Epics and epyllia were written, but surviving fragments suggest their loss is not to be regretted. That some didactic poetry has survived is due rather to its supposed usefulness than to literary merit. Dionysius of Alexandria's *Guide to the Known World* in 1186 hexameters, published in A.D. 124, is the most successful as poetry (in the Callimachean tradition) and was much read in later antiquity. Also popular then, but little read now, are the five books on fishing written later in the second century by Oppian of Cilicia, and four on hunting by a Syrian, wrongly transmitted as the work of Oppian.

A comparably small proportion of philosophical writing shows either distinction or originality. Development of most schools of thought had ceased by the end of the first century B.C. and, in an age when professors as well as students of philosophy might be eclectic, handbooks and commentaries bulked large. Exposition of established positions by a skilful writer produced some memorable literature. As well as Plutarch's moral essays we have Arrian's report of the *Lectures of Epictetus*. Four of an original twelve books survive, purporting to be a transcript of the lectures Arrian himself heard from the Stoic ex-slave at Nicopolis *c.*A.D. 108, although we may reasonably suspect that much of the form and structure is due to Arrian. The diatribe style is sharp and provocative, each question a gadfly stinging the ruminant mind of the leisured audience:

What does it matter to you which road you take to Hades? They are all the same. And if you want to hear the truth, the one a tyrant sends you is shorter. No tyrant ever executed someone for six months, but fever often has for a year. All this is mere noise and a parade of empty words.

'I'm risking my neck in Caesar's court.' And am *I* not risking mine, living in Nicopolis where there are all these earthquakes? And when you yourself are sailing across the Adriatic, what are you risking? Isn't it your neck? 'But I am also risking my beliefs.' *Your* beliefs? Who can compel you to believe something you don't want? Or do you mean someone else's? Then what danger is it to you if other people have false beliefs? 'But I risk exile.' What is exile? . . .

(Epictetus ii 6.18–22)

A similar Stoic concern with how each man should play the part allotted him in the universe infuses the *Meditations* of the emperor Marcus Aurelius. But their eleven books are closer to an anthology of philosophical aphorisms than to coherent exposition of a creed. For a near contemporary example of the latter we must turn not to a literary text but to the vast inscription (the longest known from the ancient world) erected in his Lycian home town by Diogenes of Oenoanda, impelled by disease and age to preach the philosophy of Epicurus to his citizens in a form both spectacular and enduring.

Such works attest the role of moral philosophy in society, but they ask no new questions and offer no new answers. However, in Platonism there was development. Throughout the period Plato had become increasingly influential, not least because his works were read as much for their literary as their philosophical appeal. Their streak of mysticism also appealed to readers seeking religious as well as philosophical explanations of the world and offered a bridge to another school with a new lease of life, Pythagoreanism. The consequent development, Neo-Platonism, was to have great influence in the later Middle Ages and Renaissance. Its greatest exponent, Plotinus (A.D. 204–70), is known to us from a biography by his pupil Porphyry, who was also responsible for the publication of his works. These short essays, grouped in books of nine — hence their title *Enneads* — discuss ethics, physics, psychology, cosmology, and metaphysics, often modifying Platonic positions in the light of doctrines of other schools. All constituents of our universe are seen as emanations from an ineffable and transcendent incorporeal being. The difficulty of comprehending his baffling mixture of rationality and mysticism is not eased by compressed and allusive language, yet a modern reader can see why Plotinus excited an age seeking truth on many levels of reality.

VI

The late third century marked no abrupt change in the character of Greek literature, but it did see the beginning of important changes in the historical environment in which it was produced. Between the third and the seventh centuries it was to surrender its role as the major literature of an empire stretching from Britain to the Euphrates. An early omen may be seen in the sack of Athens by the Goths in A.D. 267. First the separation of eastern and western empires and finally the loss of the western empire to barbarians significantly reduced the audience of Greek writing. The sixth-century decline of Greek cities in Syria and Asia Minor was aggravated by the Persian invasions of the early seventh century, so that by the mid-seventh century Greek had become the parochial literature of a superficially educated minority in Constantinople, capital of a shrunken empire in which city life was at an end.

Alongside the reading public's diminution in size was a change in orientation. From the early fourth century, when Constantine made Christianity the official religion of the empire, the decision to write in traditional Greek forms could represent a real choice, whether the author was pagan or Christian, and a choice which increasingly ignored the contemporary interests and structure of society. These were for the most part catered for by genres specifically Christian: some were akin to traditional pagan forms — letters, homilies, lives of saints, chronicles — others, like the gospels themselves, or like histories of the Church, have no close analogue in pagan Greek literature.

It is convenient to see the classicizing products of this era as the last monuments of Greek literature, and to group its explicitly Christian literature, even when traditional in form, with that of middle Byzantium, when paganism was no longer a factor to be reckoned with. The fourth century can still boast impressive pagan writing. Sophistic rhetoric flourished across a similar range to that of the second century, but without innovatory developments. The philosophical Themistius may be more profound than display orators like Himerius and Libanius, but few of their voluminous remains are much read, and the comparable speeches of the emperor Julian are less rewarding than his letters, or his satirical dialogue in which his predecessors on the imperial throne are mocked.

Fourth-century sophists and philosophers form the subject of a set of 'Lives' by Eunapius of Sardis (A.D. 348/9–*c.*414). They are inferior to those of his model, Philostratus, and we might have been better served by his lost history, apparently covering the period from 270 to *c.*407: but for it, as for the continuation by Olympiodorus, we have to rely on the derivative Zosimus (*fl. c.* 500), whose own historical efforts when he reached a period where he had no source to epitomize give little ground for confidence.

The sixth century saw a miniature renaissance. Historical writing flourished, and we have two monuments to the continuity of classical traditions in the works of Procopius (*fl.*A.D. 530–50) and Agathias (A.D. 536–*c.*580). Procopius is more widely read — partly for the scandalous gossip of the *Secret History* rather than the solider material of the *Wars* — and his plainer style is more typical of the majority of sixth-century historians known only from fragments; Agathias is the more accomplished writer technically, and along with other classicizing spirits in sixth-century Constantinople he practised that hardy perennial of poetry, the epigram in elegiac couplets. The final contribution to classical historiography was made by the Egyptian Theophylact Simocatta (*fl.* 610–30) in an eight-book history of the period 582–602 which accommodated some Christian elements in the traditional format.

In the third century it might have seemed that hexameter poetry was destined to remain servile to tradition. Quintus of Smyrna's account of the events at Troy between Hector's death and the departure of the Greeks is too flat and unimaginative to take many readers through all its fourteen books. Triphiodorus (*c.*A.D. 300) achieved greater effect by limiting his *Capture of Troy* to a single book. But Nonnus from Panopolis in Egypt (*fl.*450

—70?) was more ambitious and innovatory. His *Dionysiac Tales,* an epic in forty-eight books, incorporates a vast range of other legends into the story of Dionysus. Its rich, baroque language, heavy with epithet and imagery, reveals an imagination well-moulded by art, as well as technical ability in reconciling the quantitative classical hexameter with popular modes of versification based on the stress accent. Nonnus also wrote a verse paraphrase of St John's gospel. His influence is clear in Musaeus' *Hero and Leander* and Colluthus' *Rape of Helen,* both poems whose few hundred lines, written *c.*A.D. 500, are not without charm. It is still apparent in Paul the Silentiary, whose 1032 lines on Santa Sophia, recited at its rededication in 563, show originality in adapting the Nonnian model to a Christian architectural subject.

Greek literature continued to use traditional language, and often traditional forms, until Constantinople fell to the Turks in 1453. But from the sixth century its spirit was Christian rather than Greek, and the works of Nonnus and Paul, like that of Theophylact Simocatta, appropriately reflect the transition from pagan Hellenism to Byzantine Christianity.

Chronological table

Some authors (e.g. Sophocles) had extremely long active careers; others (e.g. Agathon), so far as the available evidence goes, were active for a much shorter period; others again (e.g. Thucydides) are known to us each by one work, put into the form in which we have it at the end of their lives. For the purpose of this table the approximate mid-point of an author's adult life is treated as his date. There is room for doubt and disagreement about the precise dating of authors in the archaic period and of some authors in the Hellenistic and Roman periods. Major uncertainties are indicated below by a question-mark.

B.C.	Archaic Period	
700	Hesiod*	
675	Homer*	
650	Archilochus; Semonides; Callinus; Tyrtaeus	
625		
600	Mimnermus Alcman Solon; Sappho; Alcaeus	
575		
550	Stesichorus; Hipponax Anaximander; Anaximenes	*Homeric Hymns:* various dates, 650–450 *Theognidea:* various dates, 630–450
525	Ibycus; Anacreon Xenophanes Heraclitus	
500	Simonides	

*The co-authors of this book do not all agree about the relative dating of Homer and Hesiod.

Classical Period

475	Parmenides	Persian invasion of Greece 480–479
	Epicharmus	
	Pindar; Aeschylus (d. *c.*456); Empedocles	
450	Bacchylides	
	Anaxagoras	Outbreak of Peloponnesian War 431
	Sophocles (d. 406/5); Euripides (d. 407/6); Herodotus	
425		
	Gorgias; Antiphon; Hippocrates	
	Timotheus; Agathon; Aristophanes (d. *c.*385); Thucydides	
400	Andocides	Surrender of Athens to Sparta 404
	Lysias	
375	Plato (d. 348/7)	
	Xenophon; Isocrates (d. 338); Ephorus	
350		
	ᴅemosthenes (d. 322)	Philip's victory over the Greeks 338
	Aristotle (d. 322)	Death of Alexander 323
325		

Hellenistic Period

300	Theophrastus	
	Menander; Philetas; Epicurus	
	Zeno	
275	Theocritus	
	Callimachus; Aratus; Apollonius of Rhodes	
250		
	Archimedes; Aristarchus (astronomer)	
	Eratosthenes	
225		
200		Beginnings of Roman intervention in Greece and the Aegean
175		
	Aristarchus (Homeric scholar)	
150	Polybius	Roman destruction of Corinth 146
	Panaetius	
125		

100	Meleager
75	Posidonius Parthenius
50	

Roman Period

Roman annexation of Egypt 30

25	Dionysius of Halicarnassus Strabo
A.D. 25	
50	(?) Chariton
75	Josephus Dio of Prusa Plutarch (d. *c.*120)
100	
125	
	Appian; Arrian
150	Pausanias; Aelius Aristides
175	Lucian Oppian; (?) Longus; (?) Achilles Tatius
200	Cassius Dio; Philostratus
225	Herodian
250	(?) Heliodorus; Quintus of Smyrna Plotinus
275	

300	(?) Triphiodorus	Roman Empire becomes officially Christian
325		Byzantium refounded as 'Constantinople' 324
350	Julian Libanius	
375		
400	Eunapius	
425		
450	Nonnus (?) Zosimus	
475		Final break-up of Roman Empire in Western Mediterranean
500		
525		
550	Procopius	
575	Agathias	

Further reading

Chapter 1

English translations of all Greek authors of importance are available; the principal series are the Loeb Classical Library, the Penguin Classics, and The World's Classics (Oxford University Press).

The most comprehensive up-to-date history of Greek literature is that of A. Lesky, translated by J. Willis and C. De Heer (London, 1966). A *Cambridge History of Classical Literature* is in preparation.

Chapter 2

The most successful modern verse translation of the Homeric poems is that by Robert Fitzgerald (New York, 1975). The Homeric Hymns and Hesiod are best read in the translation by H. G. Evelyn-White in the Loeb Classical Library (London, 1914; revised 1920, 1936).

Other works include:
H. Fränkel, *Early Greek Poetry and Philosophy* (Oxford, 1975)
C. M. Bowra, *Heroic Poetry* (London, 1952) and *Homer* (London, 1972)
G. S. Kirk, *The Songs of Homer* (Cambridge, 1962)
M. L. Finley, *The World of Odysseus* (Harmondsworth, 1962)
Jasper Griffin, *Homer* (Oxford, 1980)

Chapter 3

The Oxford Book of Greek Verse in Translation (Oxford, 1938) contains a generous selection from the lyric poets in verse renderings. A smaller selection, in plain prose, may be found in *The Penguin Book of Greek Verse*, edited by C. A. Trypanis (Harmondsworth, 1971). Pindar is available in a translation by C. M. Bowra, *The Odes of Pindar* (Harmondsworth, 1969).

Other works include:
H. Fränkel, as for chapter 2
C. M. Bowra, *Greek Lyric Poetry* (second edition, Oxford, 1961) and *Pindar* (Oxford, 1964)

Chapter 4

All the tragedies are to be found in translation in the Penguin Classics: Aeschylus in two volumes, Sophocles in two and Euripides in four. General introductions to Greek tragedy are numerous; among the most recent are:

H. C. Baldry, *The Greek Tragic Theatre* (London, 1971)

O. Taplin, *Greek Tragedy in Action* (London, 1978)

B. Vickers, *Towards Greek Tragedy* (London, 1973)

P. Walcot, *Greek Drama in its Theatrical and Social Context* (Cardiff, 1976).

The most important reference work is A. Lesky, *Greek Tragic Poetry* (English translation by M. Dillon, New Haven and London, 1983). There is a collection of important essays on individual plays in *Oxford Readings in Greek Tragedy*, edited by Erich Segal (Oxford, 1984).

Chapter 5

The whole of Aristophanes is available in the Penguin Classics, translated by D. Barrett and A. Sommerstein. The first volume of a new Loeb edition of Menander by W. G. Arnott has now appeared (Cambridge, Mass., and London, 1979).

For general discussion, see:

K. J. Dover, *Aristophanic Comedy* (London, Berkeley & Los Angeles, 1972)

Kenneth McLeish, *The Theatre of Aristophanes* (London, 1980)

F. H. Sandbach, *The Comic Theatre of Greece and Rome* (London, 1977)

T. B. L. Webster, *An Introduction to Menander* (Manchester, 1974).

Chapter 6

The Penguin Classics include translations of Herodotus, Thucydides, and Xenophon's *Hellenica* ('A History of my Times') and *Anabasis* ('The Persian Expedition'). General books on Herodotus and Thucydides are:

J. Hart, *Herodotus and Greek History* (London, 1982)

K. H. Waters, *Herodotus the Historian* (London, 1985)

W. Robert Connor, *Thucydides* (Princeton, 1984)

J. H. Finley, *Thucydides* (Cambridge, Mass., 1942)

F. E. Adcock, *Thucydides and his History* (Cambridge, 1963).

Chapter 7

A selection of Hippocratic writings is translated by J. Chadwick and W. N. Mann, with an introduction by G. E. R. Lloyd, in *Hippocratic Writings* (Penguin Classics). Most works of Plato, and the *Ethics, Poetics and Politics* of Aristotle, are also available in the Penguin series.

The standard reference work on the Greek philosophers in W. K. C. Guthrie's *History of Greek Philosophy* (six volumes, Cambridge, 1967-1981); two portions of it, *The Sophists* and *Socrates,* are available separately. On Aristotle see also D. J. Allan, *The Philosophy of Aristotle* (second edition, Oxford, 1970).

Chapter 8

A selection of speeches is translated by A. N. W. Saunders in *Greek Political Oratory* (Harmondsworth, 1970) and the four great speeches mentioned on p. 132, by the same translator, in *Demosthenes and Aeschines* (Harmondsworth, 1975). See also George Kennedy, *The Art of Persuasion in Greece* (Princeton and London, 1973) and Lionel Pearson, *The Art of Demosthenes* (Meisenheim, 1976).

Chapter 9

The most important books to consult for information about the Hellenistic Age include:

  J. Onians, *Art and Thought in the Hellenistic Age* (London, 1979)
  W. W. Tarn and G. T. Griffith, *Hellenistic Civilization* (London, 1952)
  T. B. L. Webster, *Hellenistic Poetry and Art* (London, 1964).

  Loeb volumes are available, with facing translations, of Theocritus, Callimachus (two volumes, one also containing Aratus and Lycophron), the Greek Anthology (five volumes), and Polybius (six volumes); also *Poems of Callimachus*, translated by R. A. Furness (London, 1931), *The Greek Bucolic Poets*, translated by A. S. F. Gow (Cambridge, 1953), and Apollonius of Rhodes, *The Voyage of Argo*, translated by E. V. Rieu (Harmondsworth, 1958). On Callimachus and Theocritus, see the last chapters of B. Snell, *The Discovery of the Mind* (Oxford, 1953).

  Other works include:
  A. A. Long, *Hellenistic Philosophy* (London, 1974)
  F. W. Walbank, *Polybius* (Berkeley, 1972)

Chapter 10

There are Loeb volumes, with facing translations, of practically all the authors named in this chapter.

  Other works include:
  B. P. Reardon, *Courants littéraires grecs des IIe et IIIe siècles après J.-C.* (Paris, 1971)
  D. A. Russell, *Plutarch* (London, 1973)
  C. P. Jones, *The Roman World of Dio Chrysostom* (Cambridge, Massachusetts, 1978)
  C. P. Jones, *Plutarch and Rome* (Oxford, 1971)
  G. W. Bowersock, *Greek Sophists in the Roman Empire* (Oxford, 1969)
  G. Anderson, *Lucian: Theme and Variation in the Second Sophistic* and *Studies in Lucian's Comic Fiction* (both Leiden, 1976)

Index

Academy, 112
Achilles, 15–18
Achilles Tatius, 170
acting, 52
Aelian, 157
Aelius Aristides, 167
Aeschines, 132
Aeschylus, 2, 51–8, 60–2, 68, 73, 81
Aethiopis, 14
afterlife, 118f.
Agamemnon, 17, 50, 53–5, 71
Agathias, 175
Agathon, 81, 116f.
Alcaeus, 39f.
Alcibiades, 110
Alcman, 40f.
Alexander the Great, 4, 131, 134
Alexandria, 134, 136, 141f., 145f., 155
Anacreon, 42f.
Anaxagoras, 118
Anaximander, 105
Anaximenes, 105
Andocides, 127
Androtion, 100
Antigone, 63f.
Antiphon (orator), 126
Antiphon (sophist), 109f.
Anyte, 148
Apollonius of Rhodes, 141–4
Apollonius of Tyana, 164
Appian, 160
Aratus of Soli, 144
Arcesilaus, 151
Archilochus, 32f.
Archimedes 135
Archytas, 111
Argentarius, 172
Argonauts, 20, 141–3
Aristarchus of Samos, 135
Aristophanes, 8, 60f., 65, 74–83
Aristotle, 6, 59–61, 112, 119–21

Arrian, 159f., 172
Asclepiades, 147
Asianism, 156, 167
Athens, 2–4, 55, 94, 96, 100–3, 122, 133, 155, 174
Atticism, 135, 156f., 160

Babylonia, 8
Bacchylides, 6, 44, 47
biography, 163f.
Bion, 141
Byzantium, 5, 7, 174f.

Callimachus, 136–9
Callinus, 35
Cassandra, 71, 145
Cassius Dio, 160f.
characterization, 65f., 85, 142f.
Chariton, 169f.
chorus, 52, 60f., 65, 74f., 82
Christianity, 3, 5, 55, 149, 174–6
chronology, 88f., 95, 113
Chrysippus (philosopher), 151
city-states, 2f., 131
Cleanthes, 151
Clytaemnestra, 53, 71
Colluthus, 176
comedy, 4, 8, 74–87
Corinth, 103
Crinagoras, 171
Critias, 110
Ctesias, 104
curses, 70

dancing, 31, 74
Daphnis, 140f.
Delphic oracle, 109, 116, 162
Democritus, 109, 149
Demosthenes, 130–3
deus ex machina, 57f.
dialect, 3, 27, 30, 40
dialogue, 113–16

didactic poetry, 25f., 144, 172
Dio of Prusa, 166f.
Diogenes of Oenoanda, 173
Dionysius of Alexandria, 172
Dionysius of Halicarnassus, 156, 158
Dionysus, 50, 57
Dorians, 76

Egypt, 2, 5, 8, 88, 90f.
Electra, 53f.
elegy, 29–31, 35–8
Empedocles, 108f., 135
Ephorus, 100f.
epic poetry, 11–24, 29f., 141–4, 172
Epicharmus, 76
Epictetus, 172f.
Epicurus, 148–50, 173
epigram, 29, 48–50, 146–8, 171f.
Erasistratus, 135
Eratosthenes, 145
Euclid, 135
Eunapius, 175
Euphorion, 145
Euripides, 51, 53, 56–8, 57f., 60,
    65–9

Fate, 18
festivals, 55
folk-tales, 20
formulae, 13

genealogy, 88, 93
geography, 158f.
gods, 17f., 22f., 71f., 84
Gorgias, 126f., 130

Hecataeus of Miletus, 91, 109
Hector, 15–18
Helen of Troy, 11, 53, 126
Heliodorus, 170
Hellanicus, 100
Hellenica of Oxyrhynchus, 100
Heraclitus of Ephesus, 109
Herakles, 58, 66f., 168f.
Herennius Dexippus, 161
Herodas, 144
Herodian, 161
Herodotus, 89–95, 98, 161f.
Heron, 135
Herophilus, 135
Hesiod, 24–8
hexameters, 139

hiatus, 113, 131
Himerius, 175
Hippocrates, 107f.
Hippolytus, 56f., 65
Hipponax, 34f.
historiography, 88–104, 152f.,
    159–61, 164
Homer, 11–22, 24, 27f., 40, 94, 122
Homeric Hymns, 23f.

iambic metre, 144
iambic poetry, 29f., 32f.
Isaeus, 133
Isocrates, 128–30

Jason, 141–3
Josephus, 159

lawcourts, 124f., 133
Leonidas of Tarentum, 148
Libanius, 175
Longus, 170f.
Lucian, 168f.
Lyceum, 120
Lycophron, 145
Lydia, 89, 93
lyric poetry, 29
Lysias, 127f.

Marcus Aurelius, 173
Medea, 60, 142f.
medicine, 107f.
Meleager of Gadara, 146, 148
melic poetry, 29–31
Menander, 6, 83–7
metaphysics, 117–19
metre, 30f.
mime, 76, 141
Mimnermus, 35f.
moralizing, 85, 99, 103f.
Moschus, 141
Musaeus, 176
music, 31, 47
Myceneans, 11f.
myth, 52, 59, 93, 168f.

Neo-Platonism, 173
Nicander, 145
Nonnus, 175f.
novel, 169f.

Odysseus, 19–22

Oedipus, 71–3
Olympic games, 44f.
Oppian, 172
oral literature, 10, 12, 14
oral tradition, 88, 92f., 95
Orestes, 53–5, 58

Palatine Anthology, 146–8
Panaetius, 152
papyrus, 2, 5f.
Parmenides, 108
Parthenius, 146
pastoral poetry, 139–41
Paul the Silentiary, 176
Pausanias, 161f.
Peloponnesian War, 94–7, 102
Pericles, 125
Persia, 2, 50, 89–92
Phaedra, 56
Philetas, 136
Philip of Macedon, 4, 128f., 131f.
philosophy, 105f., 108–20, 148–52, 162, 172
Philostratus, 164f., 175
Phrynichus (tragic poet), 53
Pindar, 29, 44–7
Plato, 110–19, 173
plot, 83
Plotinus, 173f.
Plutarch, 162–4
poetic language, 30f.
politics, 122
Polybius, 152f.
Porphyry, 173
Posidonius, 152
Posidippus, 147
Presocratics, 108
prologue, 58, 84
Prometheus, 73
prose, 10f.
Protagoras, 125
Pythagoras, 109

Quintus of Smyrna, 175

religion, 8, 54–6, 59, 62, 80, 98f., 103f., 117f.
Rome, 4, 145f., 152f., 155–7, 159, 162

Sappho, 38–40
satire, 168, 172
Second Sophistic, 165–8

self-expression, 9
Semonides, 33f.
Simonides, 43f., 49
Socrates, 77, 81, 108–20
Solon, 35–7, 70
sophists, 125
Sophocles, 51, 53f., 57f., 60, 62–7, 71f.
Sparta, 40f., 94, 101, 103
speeches, 94, 97f., 122
Stesichorus, 41f., 53
Stoics, 150–2, 172f.
Strabo, 158f.
Syracuse, 44, 76, 96f., 112

textual criticism, 6f.
theatre, 52
Thebes, 101, 103
Themistius, 175
Theocritus, 139–41
Theognis and *Theognidea*, 37f.
Theopompus, 100
Theophrastus, 121
Theophylact Simocatta, 175f.
Theseus, 56f., 66f., 72, 142
Thirty Tyrants, 127f.
Timotheus, 47f.
tragedy, 2–4, 50–73, 84
translation, 7
Triphiodorus, 175
Trojan War, 11f., 15–19, 93
Tyrtaeus, 35

values, 8f.
vase-painting, 74

war, 69, 77f.
word-order, 131
writing, 1f., 10

Xenophanes, 108, 111
Xenophon, 100–4, 110f., 156, 159

Zeno of Citium, 150f.
Zeus, 16–18, 37, 46, 151

OXFORD

OPUS

General Editors
Keith Thomas
Alan Ryan
Peter Medawar

OPUS books provide concise, original, and authoritative introductions to a wide range of subjects in the humanities and sciences. They are written by experts for the general reader as well as for students

Most of the titles listed below are available only in paperback editions; some, however, are available in both hardback and paperback, and few in hardback only. Further details of OPUS books and a complete list of Oxford Paperbacks, including The World's Classics, Twentieth-Century Classics, Past Masters, Oxford Authors, Oxford Shakespeare, and Oxford Paperback Reference, as well as OPUS, is available in the UK from the General Publicity Department, Oxford University Press, Walton Street, Oxford, OX2 6DP

In the USA, complete lists are available from the Paperbacks Marketing Manager, Oxford University Press, 200 Madison Avenue, New York, NY 10016

Architecture

The Shapes of Structure
Heather Martienssen

Business Studies

The Way People Work
Christine Howarth

Economics

The Economics of Money
A. C. L. Day

History

*The Industrial Revolution
1760–1830*
T. S. Ashton

*Karl Marx
His Life and Environment*
Isaiah Berlin

*Christianity in the West
1400–1700*
John Bossy

*Early Modern France,
1560–1715*
Robin Briggs

Modern Spain, 1875–1980
Raymond Carr

*The Workshop of the World
British Economic History from
1820–1880*
J. D. Chambers

*English Towns in Transition,
1500–1700*
Peter Clark and Paul Slack

*The Economy of England,
1450–1750*
Donald C. Coleman

*The Impact of English Towns,
1700–1800*
P. J. Corfield

*The Russian Revolution,
1917–1932*
Sheila Fitzpatrick

War in European History
Michael Howard

Roman Catholicism
E. R. Norman

England and Ireland since 1800
Patrick O'Farrell

The First World War
Keith Robbins

The French Revolution
J. M. Roberts

*The Voice of the Past
Oral History*
Paul Thompson

*Town, City, and Nation
England 1850–1914*
P. J. Waller

*Britain in the Age of Economic
Management
An Economic History since 1939*
John Wright

Law

Law and Modern Society
P. S. Atiyah

*Introduction to English Law
Revised Edition*
William Geldart

The Lawful Rights of Mankind
Paul Sieghart

Literature

The Modern American Novel
Malcolm Bradbury

*This Stage-Play World
English Literature and its
Background, 1580–1625*
Julia Briggs

Medieval Writers and their Work
English Literature and its
    Background, 1100–1500
J. A. Burrow

Romantics, Rebels and
    Reactionaries
English Literature and its
    Background, 1760–1830
Marilyn Butler

Ancient Greek Literature
Kenneth Dover and others

*Shakespeare
Philip Edwards

*Linguistic Criticism
Roger Fowler

British Theatre since 1955
Ronald Hayman

Modern English Literature
W. W. Robson

Mathematics

What is Mathematical Logic?
J. N. Crossley and others

Medical Sciences

What is Psychotherapy?
Sidney Block

Man against Disease
Preventive Medicine
J. A. Muir Gray

Philosophy

Aristotle the Philosopher
J. L. Ackrill

The Philosophy of Aristotle
D. J. Allan

*Political Theorists of the
    Enlightenment
Maurice Cranston

The Standing of Psychoanalysis
B. A. Farrell

The Character of Mind
Colin McGinn

Moral Philosophy
D. D. Raphael

The Problems of Philosophy
Bertrand Russell

Structuralism and since
From Levi-Strauss to Derrida
Edited by John Sturrock

Free Will and Responsibility
Jennifer Trusted

Ethics since 1900
Mary Warnock

Existentialism
Mary Warnock

Politics and International Affairs

Devolution
Vernon Bogdanor

Marx's Social Theory
Terrell Carver

Contemporary International
    Theory and the Behaviour of
    States
Joseph Frankel

International Relations in a
    Changing World
Joseph Frankel

The Life and Times of Liberal
    Democracy
G. B. Macpherson

The Nature of American Politics
H. G. Nicholas

English Local Government
    Reformed
Lord Redcliffe-Maud and Bruce
Wood

Religion

An Introduction to the
Philosophy of Religion
Brian Davies

Islam
An Historical Survey
H. A. R. Gibb

Religion and the People of
Western Europe
Hugh McLeod

What is Theology?
Maurice Wiles

Hinduism
R. C. Zaehner

Science

The Philosophies of Science
An Introductory Survey
R. Harre

A Historical Introduction to the
Philosophy of Science
J. P. Losee

The Problems of Biology
John Maynard Smith

The Making of the Atomic Age
Alwyn McKay

The Structure of the Universe
Jayant V. Narlikar

What is Ecology?
Denis F. Owen

Energy: A Guidebook
Janet Ramage

The Problems of Evolution
Mark Ridley

Social Sciences

Science and Technology in
World Development
Robin Clarke

Change in British Society
A. H. Halsey

Towns and Cities
Emrys Jones

Democracy at Work
Thomas Schuller

Races of Africa
C. G. Seligman

*forthcoming